Is There Life After Death?

by

Joh

Zola Levitt

ZOLA
Box 12268
Dallas, TX 75225

Other books in this series

Encounters with UFO's
The Transcendental Explosion
Psychic Healing
The Spirit of Sun Myung Moon

IS THERE LIFE AFTER DEATH?
Copyright © 1977 Harvest House Publishers
Irvine, California 92714
Copyright © 1991 Zola Levitt Ministries, Inc.
Dallas, Texas 75225
Library of Congress Catalog Card Number: 77-75410
ISBN: 0-89081-232-2

Printed in the United States of America

ABOUT THE AUTHORS

John Weldon received a B.A. degree from California State University of San Diego; an M.A. degree from Simon Greenleaf School of Law in Anaheim, California; M.Div. and D.Min. degrees from Luther Rice Seminary in Jacksonville, Florida; and M.A. and Ph.D. degrees from Pacific College of Graduate Studies in Melbourne, Victoria, Australia. He is Senior Researcher/Writer for The John Ankerberg Show and is the author of 21 books and numerous articles.

Zola Levitt, a Jewish believer, is best known as the host of the weekly national television program ZOLA LEVITT PRESENTS. He is a widely published author with some 40 books in several languages and the composer of some 100 spiritual songs. A specialist in the biblical sites, he leads several tours each year to Israel, Greece, and Egypt. He holds music degrees from Duquesne University and Indiana University, and an Honorary Th.D. from Faith Bible College.

PREFACE TO 1991 EDITION

Counterfeiting the Gospel itself, the "life after death" phenomena promise eternal life without salvation. The latter factor, however, determines our position with God—in this or the next life—and is the crucial point purposefully obscured by this attractive philosophy.

Let's face it: The "New Age" is not what it used to be. For one thing, it didn't used to be new. False doctrines, ways of avoiding God by misinterpreting Him, and downright worship of other gods have been around since the day Cain's sacrifice was rejected. The Old Testament clearly forbade the consulting of wizards and the calculating of times and the like, since they mesmerized their followers and distracted them from the real Creator God.

In New Testament times, purposeful errors based on amalgamating pagan and worldly practices with Christianity were a new distraction. Gnosticism, sacramentalism and other common errors of doctrine were replete throughout the Roman Empire and Medieval Europe, with some errors surviving today. Replacement Theology, for example, is as old as St. Augustine.

Finally, in our own day, we confront myriad cults, many based on a leavening of Biblical principles with Eastern mysticism, modern science and even Satan worship.

This series of books about cultic worship deals with five of the most popular modern errors: the UFO phenomenon covered in *Encounters with UFO's*; the world of meditation in *The Transcendental Explosion*; the quasi-Christian type of cult in *The Spirit of Sun Myung Moon*; the remarkable world of supposed experiences in the hereafter in *Is There Life After Death?*; and the myriad quasi-religious philosophies of healing in *Psychic Healing.*

These aren't necessarily the only cults or "New Age" beliefs that might be chronicled, but if I wrote about them all, in the words of John, ". . .I suppose that even the world itself could not contain the books that should be written" (John 21:25).

What is now referred to as the "New Age Movement" is simply an update of all of the unbelief of all of the ages since the garden. The alternative ways to God prepared by the various "New Age" gods of today represent many of the same fallacies as those of yesterday. A working knowledge of the subjects of this five-book series will arm any believer against the father of all cults, the "prince of this world."

TABLE OF CONTENTS

"The last enemy that will be abolished is death."

I Corinthians 15 : 26

1

The Wonderful World of Death

I had a heart attack, and I found myself in a black void, and I knew I had left my physical body behind, I knew I was dying. . .I was moved out of that blackness, through a pale gray, and I just went on, gliding and moving swiftly, and in front of me, in the distance, I could see a gray mist, and I was rushing toward it. It seemed that I just couldn't get to it fast enough to satisfy me, and as I got closer to it I could see through it. Beyond the mist, I could see people, and their forms were just like they are on the earth, and I could also see something which one could take to be buildings. The whole thing was permeated with the most gorgeous light — a living, golden yellow glow, a pale color, not like the harsh gold color we know on earth.

As I approached more closely, I felt certain that I was going through that mist. It was such a wonderful, joyous feeling; there are just no words, in human language to describe it. Yet, it wasn't my time to go through the mist, because instantly from the other side appeared my Uncle Carl, who had died many years earlier. He blocked my path, saying, "Go back. Your work on earth has not been completed. Go back now." I didn't want to go back, but I had no choice, and immediately I was back in my body. I felt that horrible pain in my chest.[1]

That was the testimony of a young mother who had taken today's most fascinating "trip." She had left her body, taken a look at what she would undoubtedly describe as "The Wonderful World of Death," and then returned. She wasn't overly happy about resuming this earthly existence.

Another young lady "died" while enduring a difficult birth. This one confronted a welcoming committee on "the other side."

I had this experience when I was giving birth to a child. The delivery was very difficult, and I lost a lot of blood. The doctor gave me up, and told my relatives that I was dying. However, I was quite alert through the whole thing, and even as I heard him saying this I felt myself coming to. As I did, I realized that all these people were there, almost in multitudes it seems, hovering around the ceiling of the room. They were all people I had known in my past life, but who had passed on before. I recognized my grandmother and a girl I had known when I was in school, and many other relatives and friends. It seems that I mainly saw their faces and felt their presence. They all seemed pleased. It was a very happy occasion, and I felt that they had come to protect or to guide me. It was almost as if I were coming home, and they were there to greet or to welcome me. All this time I had the feeling of everything light and beautiful. It was a beautiful and glorious moment.[2]

This lady, too, was obviously not completely pleased about rejoining us in this present life. Given a choice she might well have decided to remain dead, as it were, in view of the pleasant surroundings and the good company.

There are many such stories circulating nowadays and we'll look at further cases at the end of this chapter. But first we would like to examine this strange new phenomenon in some detail. It seems that people are coming back from the dead, or at least testifying to that experience under clinical conditions.

People are dying as usual — but now some of them live to tell about it!

PEOPLE ARE DYING TO KNOW!

There is a new interest and openness today about the world's most fearsome mystery — where we go when we die. Invariably a taboo topic, death has lately come into its own as a conversation piece. Books are appearing one after the other, purporting to explain the inexplicable, and folks who have returned from the beyond are publicly willing to discuss their tours.

Even in the schools death has become okay. College and high school instructors teaching classes about death have taken their students to funeral parlors. There the students can do what they probably will never do again — lie down in a coffin alive.

Even scientists are talking seriously about death, conducting research and inquiring into a real frontier of human life. *Psychology Today* points out:

Death is in vogue as a topic of books, seminars, scholarly articles and classes at every level from college down to elementary school.[3]

A recent Gallup Poll reported that 73% of Americans believe in life after death,[4] and that large majority obviously has a more than routine interest in death.

Everybody is concerned about death. Death is one of the few topics that can truly be called "of general interest." There just are no exceptions. Humanists, communists, agnostics, theists and atheists are all very interested in death. They may have varying explanations of death, but they all try to explain it.

In this world of uncertainty death is something you can really count on. It is inevitable — final. Even the reluctance to talk about it — the longtime taboo — betrays an underlying concern. It's truly the skeleton in the closet of the whole human race. We all must face it — every last one of us.

The current interest is certainly justified. It *is* important. We all want to know exactly what death is, *why* it is, and what it will bring to us. Is there more later on, after death, or can we accurately say, "What you see is what you get!"?

It seems that very few of us want to die. People experiencing the joys of living just don't want to stop. Even people *not* experiencing joy in their lives still want to go on living. Some people are having their bodies frozen after death in the hope that science will one day discover the cure for their particular malady and thaw them out into a great new world. In the hit movie "Sleeper," an enthusiastic Woody Allen popped out of aluminum foil to confront the world a few centuries hence, with mixed blessings.

Some people kill themselves, of course, and it is not very clear in most cases what they expected to encounter. Suicides either assume that the next world will be better, or that nothing could be worse than what they have. They "end it all," with the meaning that they really expect nothing more.

But for the rest of us, our questions persist and the inevitable appointment we must keep with death hangs over us every day of our lives.

Death has successfully eluded man's scientific inquiry. We know abundantly little about this matter that concerns us all.

But we have made some guesses. Various views about death do exist, for what they're worth. The trouble is, the opinions are all expressed by live people who apparently haven't been there.

To the materialistic thinker death represents complete annihilation, non-existence. Death is the end and that's all there is to that. To many Hindus and Buddhists it represents complete absorption into the divine consciousness, or cyclic reincarnations. The Eastern thinker (and some Westerners as well) holds that he may well be back, but as someone, or something, else. It's not exactly a round trip ticket, this reincarnation. Bible-reading people hold to an eternal life of the present personality, a more comfortable thought by far. They depend on the scriptures and the very complete biblical explanations of life and death.

In the views where the present personality is done away with, either by obliteration or by reincarnation, we're somehow disappointed. People just aren't satisfied with the idea of being vanquished from this existence forever. Of course, the reincarnation folks try to look on the bright side; clergyman Leslie Weatherhead asks plaintively,

> "...would it really matter if I were lost like a drop of water in the ocean, if I could be one shining particle in some glorious wave that broke in utter splendour and in perfect beauty on the shores of an eternal sea?[5]

Poetic, but somehow unsatisfying. We don't really want to be pretty drops of water. We want to be *who we are*. Even after we expire, we want to be *us*.

Columbia University logics professor James Hyslop complains that,

It is difficult to understand what can recommend the doctrine of reincarnation, because it does not satisfy the only instinct that makes survival of any kind interesting: namely the instinct to preserve the consciousness of personal identity. A future life must be the continuity of this consciousness or it is not a life to us at all. [6]

Man longs, yearns, for a life after death that includes *himself*, his same personality with its hopes, dreams and challenges. He understands that survival after death without his own personality is meaningless, and not really survival at all. Man's innate desire to know — to solve this question of what will happen after death — has spawned the recent, almost mystical research into cases of "life after death."

Some of our fellow travelers have apparently been dead and they have a great deal to say. By carefully comparing their reports, some people have tried to inquire into this most mysterious of all human inquiries.

THE SHAKESPEARIAN CONNECTION

Psychiatrist Elizabeth Kubler-Ross is one of the world's leading authorities on death. The author of several definitive works on this subject, she is considered by many to be, if we may say so, the final word.

After her examinations of more than 1,000 clients with something really new to say about dying, Dr. Kubler-Ross sums up:

> The common denominators before they die are they are at peace; they are fully awake; when they float out of their bodies they are without fear, pain or anxiety; and they have a sense of wholeness. [7]

This psychiatrist, along with an increasing number of serious scientists, is busily gathering the testimonies of those who have taken that strange trip over the edge, and back again.

Dr. Raymond Moody, whose fascinating cases we quoted at the beginning of this chapter, currently has a book on the best-seller list called, *Life After Life.* It details the experiences of some 50 subjects who have been near death, or "clinically dead," and then revived. Moody has been "swamped with calls" offering more testimonies of the life-after-life experience since his book came out. He has followed with a sequel, *Reflections on Life After Life*, and there are seemingly still more cases to describe.

Minister Archie Matson's book, *After Life — Reports From the Threshold of Death*, leans toward occult sources for its material. That this entire subject has a certain occultic feel to it is obvious and we shall examine that in a later chapter.

The Romeo Error takes its clever title from Shakespeare and the unfortunate misjudgment the stricken Romeo made over the apparently lifeless body of Juliet. The author, Lyall Watson, examines the scientific findings on cases of reincarnation, spirit possession, astral projection (spacial "traveling") and other spiritistic phenomena. Juliet, to be fair to playwright Shakespeare, was drugged, not spiritually possessed in any way. But Lady Capulet asserted, "Her blood is settled and her joints are stiff. Life and these lips have long been separated," and Romeo killed himself in despair.

Such verifications have been made in more up-to-date language in hospital rooms, with some surprise endings.

There is some scientific confusion about death, to say the least. Death used to be defined physiologically, and was not overly difficult to diagnose; but with modern improvements in rescue and resuscitation techniques "dead" people are being "brought back." Scientists are baffled when competent doctors certify

7

a patient as clinically dead and then that patient sits up and says, "Can I go home now?" Understandably, some consternation has been caused in medical circles about these increasing reports.

Obviously, the idea of life after death has profound implications in medical, legal, scientific, social and theological areas, and a lot of people are becoming quite concerned.

From time immemorial, occultists and mediums have been saying that people lived on after they passed away from this life, and seances have "demonstrated" the phenomenon. Folks have been put in touch with dead relatives for a fee, and this is commonplace, though understandably suspect.

But only in the past ten years or so have serious scientists contemplated these mystical possibilities. The field of parapsychology, which studies ESP and other psychic phenomena, has interested researchers from many disciplines, and today hundreds of scientists are involved in what was once considered entirely outside the realm of science.

A sampling of some contemporary book titles serves to show a new found relationship between science and the psychic world: Thelma Moss' *The Probability of the Impossible*, and Lawrence Blair's, *Rhythms of Vision*, marry science and the occult; *The Tao of Physics*, by Fritjof Capra, and *Magic: Science of the Future*, by Joseph Goodavage, speak for themselves.

Bible prophecy forecasts an increase of occultic phenomena in the latter days, which some construe to represent our time. In any case, it is surprising, and perhaps disconcerting, to see some of the scientific community involved with "magic," "the Tao," and the like.

But then again, how shall we adequately explain dead people coming back to life?

GRAVE NEW WORLD

Think of the implications! Just imagine how things would change if it were scientifically established that people really do live on after death.

If life does go on after death — and a better life at that — will we start having less regard for our lives here and now? How will the practice of medicine be affected if the patient comes in with an eagerness to die and a loathing of being kept alive and ill?

What about religion? Few seem to ever refer to encountering anything like the biblical heaven or hell when they take that strange trip. If the existence of the soul is proven — if there is something there that is extra-physical that leaves the body upon death — how will that make us think about ourselves. How will we feel looking into the mirror?

And if people start believing that all the dead are still out there somewhere, "alive," or at least within reach what will happen to our society? Consider: people may come to believe that the entire community of dead persons — all who have ever lived on earth — are available to us. That includes your family, the great figures of history, the departed friends you loved. Wouldn't such an idea change the world?

Would such beliefs, in turn, cause a great upsurge in spiritual interest? Would the mediums, or some improved form of them in keeping with this "scientific age," have a field day? Would people everywhere want to "get in touch" with the "dead"?

The mind boggles.

What people believe about death tends to greatly influence how they conduct their lives. We live to a great extent in the steady consciousness that we are going to die, and probably each of us has developed some vague idea of what will go on then.

Our understanding of death and its aftermath has everything to do with our understanding of life and its meaning. Perhaps no understanding is more important.

But before we look further at that subject, let us first sample some especially provocative and fascinating cases taken from the works of Moody and Kubler-Ross. The variety, apparent veracity, and downright incredibility of the following stories will at least entertain the reader, to say nothing of sending a few chills up and down his spine.

So sit back, and keep calm.

REPORTS FROM THE HEREAFTER

Dr. Moody has created a "composite" death experience which incorporates the several elements common to most of his cases. Naturally, not every life-after-death report contains all of these elements, but the following "ideal" or "complete" experience presents the most usual order of events.

A man is dying and, as he reaches the point of greatest physical distress, he hears himself pronounced dead by his doctor. He begins to hear an uncomfortable noise, a loud ringing or buzzing, and at the same time feels himself moving very rapidly through a long dark tunnel. After this, he suddenly finds himself outside of his own physical body, but still in the immediate physical environment, and he sees his own body from a distance, as though he is a spectator. He watches the resuscitation attempt from this unusual vantage point and is in a state of emotional upheaval.

After a while, he collects himself and becomes more accustomed to his odd condition. He notices that he still has a "body," but one of a very different nature and with very different powers from the physical body he has left behind. Soon other things begin to happen. Others come to meet and to help him. He glimpses the spirits of relatives and friends who have already died, and a loving, warm spirit of a kind he has never encountered before — a being of light — appears before him. This being asks him a question,

10

nonverbally, to make him evaluate his life and helps him along by showing him a panoramic, instantaneous playback of the major events of his life. At some point he finds himself approaching some sort of barrier or border, apparently representing the limit between earthly life and the next life. Yet, he finds that he must go back to the earth, that the time for his death has not yet come. At this point he resists, for by now he is taken up with his experiences in the afterlife and does not want to return. He is overwhelmed by intense feelings of joy, love, and peace. Despite his attitude, though, he somehow reunites with his physical body and lives.

Later he tries to tell others, but he has trouble doing so. In the first place, he can find no human words adequate to describe these unearthly episodes. He also finds that others scoff, so he stops telling other people. Still, the experience affects his life profoundly, especially his views about death and its relationship to life. [8]

And that's the pristine life-after-death experience. Not everyone goes through all of the above phenomena but over a broad survey of the reported cases all of these strange things seem to happen. It's really quite a trip.

Now we can examine particular cases that are representative. One young man in a car accident reported this experience:

It was about two years ago, and I had just turned nineteen. I was driving a friend of mine home in my car, and as I got to this particular intersection downtown, I stopped and looked both ways, but I didn't see a thing coming. I pulled on out into the intersection and as I did, I heard my friend yell at the top of his voice. When I looked, I saw a blinding light, the headlights of a car that was speeding towards us. I heard this awful sound — the side of the car being crushed in — and there was just an instant during which I seemed to be going through a darkness, an enclosed space. It was very quick. Then, I was sort of floating about five feet above the street, about five yards away from the car, I'd say, and I heard the echo of the crash dying away. I saw people come running up and crowding around the car, and I saw my friend get out of the car, obviously in shock. I could see my own body in the wreckage among all those people, and could see them trying to get it out. My legs were all twisted and there was blood all over the place.[9]

A young woman expresses her bafflement at being dead, and yet alive:

I thought I was dead, and I wasn't sorry that I was dead, but I just couldn't figure out where I was supposed to go. My thought and my consciousness were just like they are in life, but I just couldn't figure all this out. I kept thinking, "Where am I going to go? What am I going to do?" and "My God, I'm dead! I can't believe it!" Because you never really believe, I don't think, fully that you're going to die. It's always something that's going to happen to the other person, and although you know it you really never believe it deep down...And so I decided I was just going to wait until all the excitement died down and they carried my body away, and try to see if I could figure out where to go from there.[10]

Another young man recalls meeting a passed-on friend upon his own death:

12

Several weeks before I nearly died, a good friend of mine, Bob, had been killed. Now the moment I got out of my body, I had the feeling that Bob was standing there, right next to me. I could see him in my mind and felt like he was there, but it was strange. I didn't see him as his physical body. I could see things, but not in the physical form, yet just as clearly, his looks, everything. Does that make sense? He was there but he didn't have a physical body. It was kind of like a clear body, and I could sense every part of it — arms, legs, and so on — but I wasn't *seeing* it physically. I didn't think about it being odd at the time because I didn't really need to see him with my eyes. I didn't have eyes, anyway.

I kept asking him, "Bob, where do I go now? What has happened? Am I dead or not?" And he never answered me, never said a word. But, often, while I was in the hospital, he would be there, and I would ask him again, "What's going on?", but never any answer. And then the day the doctors said, "He's going to live," he left. I didn't see him again and didn't feel his presence. It was almost as though he were waiting until I passed that final frontier and then he would tell me, would give me the details on what was going on. [11]

Dr. Kubler-Ross reports on a woman, who, like most undergoing the "death experience," really didn't want to be brought back:

She described the patient as a woman in her late 40's, seriously ill and alone in her hospital room. "The patient saw a nurse come in, take a look at her, and dash out. Then she floated out of her body. She floated a few feet above her body and watched her corpse in the bed. She was surprised at how pale she looked. She had this beautiful feeling of peace and equanimity. Then she watched the resuscitation team come in, and she described to me in minute detail who came into the room, what they did to her body, who behaved how, who was sent in to tell the resuscitation crew what to do, very specific detailed things. She had no vital signs — no heartbeat, no blood pressure, no respiration. She had this urgent need to tell them to relax, take it easy, let go. She was almost frantically trying to convey to them that 'It's O.K., it's beautiful.' In her words, 'The harder I tried, the more frantic they became.' In my language, the longer she didn't respond, the more they tried to bring her around. Then, again in her language, which is actually a lack of language to describe these events, she 'lost consciousness.' When she regained it, she was again lying in her hospital bed.''[12]

Dr. Moody gives an example of the ''Being of Light,'' a next-world personality encountered in many of these experiences:

I knew I was dying and that there was nothing I could do about it, because no one could hear me...I was out of my body, there's no doubt about it, because I could see my own body there on the operating room table. My soul was out! All this made me feel very bad at first, but then, this really bright light came. It did seem that it was a little dim at first, but then, it was this huge beam. It was just a tremendous amount of light, nothing like a big bright flashlight, it was just too much light. And it gave off heat to me; I felt a warm sensation.

It was a bright yellowish white — more white. It was tremendously bright; I just can't describe it. It seemed that it covered everything, yet it didn't prevent me from seeing everything around me — the operating room, the doctors and nurses, everything. I could see clearly, and it wasn't blinding.

At first, when the light came, I wasn't sure what was happening, but then, it asked, it kind of asked me if I was ready to die. It was like talking to a person, but a person wasn't there. The light's what was talking to me, but in a *voice*.

Now, I think that the voice that was talking to me actually realized that I wasn't ready to die. You know, it was just kind of testing me more than anything else. Yet, from the moment the light spoke to me, I felt really good — secure and loved. The love which came from it is just unimaginable, indescribable. It was a fun person to be with! And it has a sense of humor, too — definitely![13]

Dr. Moody also discusses several cases of the "review," a recap of the dead one's life that sometimes occurs on the "other side":

While I was serving in Viet Nam, I received wounds, and I later 'died' from them, yet through it all I knew exactly what was going on. I was hit with six rounds of machine gun fire, and as it happened, I wasn't upset at all. In my mind, I actually felt relieved when I was wounded. I felt completely at ease, and it was not frightening.

At the point of impact, my life began to become a picture in front of me, and it seemed that I could go back to the time when I was still a baby, and the pictures seemed to progress through my whole life.

I could remember everything; everything was so vivid. It was so clear in front of me. It shot right by me from the earliest things I can remember right on up to the present, and it was not anything bad at all; I went through it with no regrets, no derogatory feelings about myself at all.

The best thing I can think of to compare it to is a series of pictures, like slides. It was just like someone was clicking off slides in front of me, very quickly.[14]

Another man in a car accident was not injured at all but still encountered the "review," seemingly resulting from the shock involved:

The truck was a total wreck, but I didn't receive a scratch. Somehow, I had jumped out the front windshield, because all the glass was blown out. After things calmed down, I thought it was strange that these things that had happened in my life, that had made some sort of lasting impression on me, had gone through my mind during this moment of crisis. I could probably think of all those things and remember and picture each of them now, but it would probably take me at least fifteen minutes. Yet, this had all come at once, automatically, and in less than a second. It was amazing.[15]

Almost without exception, the life-after-death experiences take away the fear of death. This is easily seen from the above cases. Dr. Moody observes:

"In some form or another, almost every person has expressed to me the thought that he is no longer afraid of death."[16]

O DEATH, WHERE IS THY STING?

Truly, as Dr. Moody has noted, people are becoming less afraid of death — especially those who have been there. The apostle Paul, too, exulted over the defeat of death by the Lord's promise of eternal life: "O death, where is thy sting? O grave, where is thy victory?" (1 Cor. 15:55 KJV). Paul, like those who have provided the eyewitness information about the beyond, had good reason to feel that he would triumph over death and he was no longer afraid of it.

But apart from those whose religious faith sustains them, even in the face of death, most people do fear dying. Or at least that was true of most people until the recent reports from the hereafter. As matters now stand, a lot of people are rethinking death. We are getting new impressions about what death might really mean for each of us through this new research.

Conceivably there has been a recent change in what was once termed, "The American Way of Death."

(Note: A reference is given fully only in its first use.)

1. Raymond Moody, *Life After Life*, (Covington, Ga.: Mockingbird) 1975, p. 56-7.
2. Ibid., p. 44.
3. *Psychology Today*, Sept. 1976, p. 44.
4. *National Observer*, May 15, 1976, p. 10.
5. Leslie Weatherhead, *The Case For Reincarnation*, (Surrey, England: M. C. Peatro Pub.) p. 19.
6. Suzy Smith, *Suzy Smith's Supernatural World*, (McFadden-Bartell, 1971) p. 176.
7. *National Observer*, May 15, 1976, p. 10.
8. Moody, *Life After Life*, p. 23-4.
9. Ibid., p. 32-3.
10. Ibid., p. 35-6.
11. Ibid., p. 44.
12. Interview with Dr. Kubler-Ross in Feb. 1977, *Fate* Magazine, p. 68. Used by special permission.
13. Moody, *Life After Life*, p. 49-50.
14. Ibid., p. 53.
15. Ibid., p. 54.
16. Ibid., p. 68.

"In the past few years more wholesome attitudes toward death have begun to emerge. Many people now view death as an integral part of life, as a time of transition similar to other turning points of life (such as graduation, marriage, childbirth) when old ways of living end and new ways of being begin. Countless books and magazine articles have appeared on the dying process, and people are now discussing the subject more openly and with less apprehension."

Rick Ingrasci, M. D. *New Age Journal*
May, 1977, p. 87

"The quality of life is more important than life itself."

Alexis Carrel,
Living Quotation for Christians, p. 144

2

The New American Way of Death

The American Way of Death was a British-authored best-seller a few years ago that poked some fun at the way the people of the U.S. carried on about funerals. *The Loved One* was a similar exercise in ghoulish humor. It seemed that the citizens of this nation had a thing about death and gave it some very special treatment.

That the subject actually lent itself to humor, and also serious analysis, by foreign authors spoke for the fact that we did not feel very comfortable about death in this country. We did behave rather excessively, and perhaps still do, in regard to our funerals — creating some remarkable pageantry when the funds are available. And we have always, like many other peoples, attached a depth of supernatural significance to death — this thing that happens to every one of us.

Lately, our behavior toward death has taken some very peculiar turns, leading to this newest secular hope of life after death. We have perhaps begun to devalue life in the here-and-now in favor of contemplating the beyond. We have gathered like vultures around the public spectacles involved with such life and death debates as the cases of Gary Gilmore and Karen Ann Quinlan, as if each of us had a vested interest in whether those two survived or not. We have been expressing new and widely varied views about the afterlife and how to get there.

Very definitely, our national attitudes toward death have become more inquisitive and more varied, as though we are looking for a solution to this ultimate dilemma. The *new* American way of death should be examined thoroughly before we progress to investigating the ins and outs of those fascinating reports of the folks who have returned to us from the beyond.

In many societies around the world, people seem much less concerned about death and even about life. We have generally been used to more greatly valuing each human life than are the "transcendental" societies comprising an important part of the world. (But the reader might look at *The Transcendental Explosion*, by the authors, especially chapter six, "The Manson Factor," for some eye-opening American lack of concern about death, or more accurately, murder.)

Most of the readers of this book will react with sadness to facts like the following:

> ...since 3600 B.C., the world has known only 292 years of peace. In this period of more than 55 centuries, there have been 14,531 wars, large and small, in which more than 3.6 billion people were killed.[1]

But a devout Hindu of the tradition of Shakara, India's dominant view, will not be at all troubled by the above news. Death is of no importance in such circles, and in fact may be considered just an illusion — possibly an advancement into the next life.

Maharishi Mahesh Yogi, the Americanized inventor of Transcendental Meditation, would be completely unruffled. He says, 'Death as such only causes a temporary pause in the process of evolution...(and) is no real danger to life.''[2] Maharishi asks, "Can there be grief in the mind of a wise man either for the living or for the dead?"[3]

The Manson family held death in great contempt, in keeping with their Eastern views of things transcendental. Family member Leslie Van Houten stated in an interview with Barbara Walters, Jan. 27, 1977[4] that she had not felt any grief or remorse or guilt over the murders she committed because she truly believed that death wasn't real or significant. Manson disciple Susan Atkins "loved to talk about murder — the more you do it, the better you like it."[5]

The master himself, soft-spoken Charles Manson, had utterly wiped out of the minds of those girls what is considered a normal view of life and death. In his opinion death "was no more important than eating an ice cream cone."[6]

TO BE OR NOT TO BE

Karen Ann Quinlan and Gary Gilmore are two personalities familiar to almost every American. Months dragged by as the families of these singular news items, the individuals themselves and the public tried to decide whether they should live or die.

Hamlet contemplated his monumental question of whether to be or not to be privately; Gilmore and Miss Quinlan were paraded before the public in a macabre debate over life and/or death. And, obviously, the public became fascinated with the struggle. One might say that those unique personalities — one drugged into oblivion and the other convicted of multiple murders — were riding the new wave of public interest in death.

One of them was alive, but for all practical purposes was really dead. Miss Quinlan was unable to react to her own situation.

The other was alive, but *wanted* to be dead. And he was nearly denied his wish.

Doctors, lawyers, the courts and the media followed along like so many predators as the two cases progressed. Gilmore and the family representatives of Miss Quinlan got their respective wishes, as things happened, but not before the American public was made acutely conscious of some unusual angles in the process of departing this life.

The two people in these cases brought different questions to the public mind. With Miss Quinlan, there were extraordinary medical procedures in progress to sustain her life — even as her parents pressed the courts for a merciful death. The legal people were wrestling with the question of whether Miss Quinlan, utterly incapacitated as she was, were not already legally dead. The larger question, and one that we will examine in the next chapter, is this: *What constitutes death?* Miss Quinlan, functioning by machine though she was, represented one of those "clinically dead" people, and her case deeply perplexed the public. It would have been hard, at the height of discussion in that case, to get a solid public opinion on whether Miss Quinlan was still "alive," let alone whether she ought to have been allowed to "die," or continúe dying.

The Gilmore case brings up a still more fascinating question which we will deal with immediately: *What is the meaning of death?*

BLOOD ATONEMENT

Gilmore wanted to die so that he would be aquitted of his murders. He sought forgiveness in death.

He differed in an important way from Charles Manson. Manson thought death, and therefore murder, had no meaning; Gilmore attached a very profound meaning to murder and he sought atonement for his crimes. The Utah convict desperately

22

wanted to be executed because he feared drastic punishment in the afterlife if he did not pay for his crimes in this life.

Gilmore was a remarkable example of how thoroughly one's behavior is conditioned by one's concept of life after death. He believed completely in the next world — in life after death — and he particularly believed in the Mormon doctrine of personal blood atonement.[7] His life in this world was hopelessly compromised, in his view, and if he had gotten a sentence of life imprisonment, rather than the death sentence, it would have meant a hideous next-life for him.

From where he stood in this life, Gary Gilmore had everything to gain by taking his medicine (death) and going on to better things. Thus, he insisted upon the firing squad.

The Mormon Church is a peculiarly American institution, though there are other religious societies around the world who hold to personal atonement to avoid punishment after death. Sacrifice by the sinful one in order to gain a better reincarnation is a staple of the Indian sects and many tribal religions. It should be said that Mormonism no longer practices such excesses as the putting to death of extreme sinners, but Gilmore was orthodox enough to give his very life for the principle.

His particular belief in life after death literally killed him!

Brigham Young, the second president of the Mormon Church, taught:

> There are sins that men commit for which they cannot receive forgiveness in this world …and if they had their eyes open to see their true condition, they would be perfectly willing to have their blood spilt upon the ground …as an offering for their sins…I know when you hear my brethren telling about cutting people off from the earth that you consider it

strong doctrine, *but it is to save them, not to destroy them* (emphasis ours). [8]

The list of unforgiveable sins from which the church fathers wanted to ''save'' the parishioners was long. It was enough to make one want to change churches: murder (paradoxically), adultery, covenant breaking, immorality, stealing, using the name of the Lord in vain, rejecting the gospel, marrying a black person, apostasy, lying and counterfeiting.

Preacher Young unabashedly threatened his flock with extinction for turning their backs on this hard teaching. A man would be ''hewn down'' for his sins; [9] liars ''would have their heads cut off.''[10] But it was all to be done for love:

> This is loving our neighbor as ourselves; if he needs help, help him; and if he wants salvation and it is necessary to spill his blood on the earth in order that he might be saved, spill it...That is the way to love mankind.[11]

Jedediah M. Grant, Second Counselor to Young, gave the power of life and death to the Mormon leaders:

> It is their right to baptize a sinner to save him and it is also their right to kill a sinner to save him...we would not kill a man, of course, unless we killed him to save him. [12]

The Mormon Church today denies these past excesses, but former Mormons Gerald and Sandra Tanner have documented the above statements from their original sources and shown conclusively that many people were slain because of this arcane belief.[13]

Now we can more readily understand why Gary Gilmore wanted to die, and we can perceive that the view of life conditions an individual's view of death. Gilmore believed these doctrines implicitly. His own death, he felt, would turn out to be a blessing.

If Gilmore were to make it in the next life and avoid ultimate punishment, he would have to pay more now than just life imprisonment. The Los Angeles Times concluded, "Gilmore believed...that one who has shed innocent blood must likewise have his own blood shed."[14]

Gary Gilmore was scared of the next life. He was literally scared to death.

GILMORE OUR HERO

We are not so much concerned here with the theology of the Mormon Church or what Gary Gilmore believed. But what does catch our interest is the public reaction to all this.

Gary Gilmore became a hero! He was lionized.[15]

And this seems to indicate a change in our society. There is something of the new American way of death here. We seem to be moving ever closer to a Manson view of death — that it doesn't matter. Perhaps we are coming to believe in some kind of life after death, as a society, or perhaps we have become jaded in our taste for ever more delectable violence. But whatever the case, Gary Gilmore was made into some kind of folk legend, and forgiveness, which he believed was unavailable in this life, ironically poured in from all sides.

Ron Stranger, Gilmore's attorney, broke into tears with the information that his client was "A good man that loved children." A song, "The Ballad of Gary Gilmore," has been released by a Utah singing group. A book and a TV movie are both in preparation at this writing.

The public seemed to polarize on the Gilmore issue, but the forces of forgiveness and pity hit the front pages at the time of the execution. During the long night prior to the firing squad, people demonstrated against the execution and ministers held an all-night vigil of prayer that the hero might be spared. Gilmore received some 7,000 letters including the following praise from a young woman:

Dearest Gary,

I admire you very much. I think you are a brave man to want to die, I adore, love and respect and worship you very much...I hate to see such a very handsome man die... ...You're so manly, very masculine...appealing...Good luck in the other world.[16]

The excited writer above seemed to believe, like Manson, Maharishi and Gilmore himself, that the next life held better things for the condemned one. She hated to see Gilmore die because he was handsome, not because he would suffer or be gone forever.

It expresses a trend in this country toward more lenient views of murder and more sympathy for the murderer. Gilmore was, after all, a killer, and the testimony of his rampage horrifies reasonable people. But we are becoming very hardened about the human condition. We don't care so much anymore when people are killed. Perhaps like the correspondent above we're beginning to count on "Good luck in the other world."

It is not clear just how much the belief in another life to come has to do with our devaluation of the life here and now, but we are becoming calloused. Our latest policies on abortion and euthanasia, our casual acceptance of suicide and our leniency toward criminals reflect a formerly uncharacteristic attitude toward the sanctity and dignity of each human life. We used to think that each human being was precious, and if there was a life to come, so much the better. But now human life is expendable, and somehow, the "next world" will supply some good luck.

True, if we progress to a different view of death — thinking of it as a passport to some other stage of existence which we will like better when we try it — then our social fabric changes somewhat. The published "clinical death" experiences, showing people coming back to life with glowing reports from the beyond, tend to make some people think seriously about making a very big change. Dr. Kubler-Ross is concerned that some people may elect to *commit suicide* as a result of sampling the enthusiastic endorsements of life after death.[17]

Gary Gilmore, in his way, was one of those people.

WHAT IS DEATH?

We need a new definition of death.

With the social opinions about death changing, with people who are certified as dead coming back to life and with condemned criminals looking upon execution as a preferred alternative, we truly need to redefine death.

If we're all going to experience this thing, we ought to know what it's all about.

In the next chapter we will attempt what the courts and the medical people are having quite a bit of trouble with; we will try to arrive at a workable definition of death which will cover all cases, including those strange new cases. Of course we will not arrive at a definition on our own, but will present research from those who wrestle with this unique new problem. The reader is forewarned that in the light of the latest developments, this subject has become very complex.

Death is just not what it used to be.

1. *Stockton Record*, (Stockton, Calif. newspaper) from an issue between March 13-18, 1960 or March 3-8, 1963.
2. Maharishi M. Yogi, *On The Bhagavad Gita*, (Baltimore: Penguin Books) 1969, p. 233.
3. Ibid., p. 90.
4. "The Goodnight America Show" with Geraldo Riveras, 10:30 p.m.
5. Vincent Bugliosi, *Helter Skelter*, (New York: Bantam) 1975, p. 129.
6. Ibid., p. 301.
7. *Los Angeles Times*, Jan. 17-18, 1977.
8. Gerald and Sandra Tanner, *Mormonism: Shadow or Reality*, p. 398 (Salt Lake City: Modern Microfilm Co.) 1972, from Box 1884 Salt Lake City, Utah 84110. Quote is from *Journal of Discourses*, Vol. 4, p. 53-4. All Mormonism quotes are from Ch. 25 "Blood Atonement."
9. Ibid., p. 401, from *Journal of Discourses*, Vol. 3, p. 226; Vol. 10, p. 110.

10. Tanner, p. 402, from ''Manuscript History of Brigham Young,'' Dec. 20, 1846.
11. Tanner, p. 402, from *Deseret News*, Feb. 18, 1857; *Journal of Discourses*, Vol. 4, p. 219-20.
12. Tanner, p. 402, from *Deseret News*, July 27, 1854.
13. See all of Ch. 25, ''Blood Atonement,'' note 8.
14. *Los Angeles Times*, Jan. 18, 1977.
15. Ibid., and Jan. 17, 1977.
16. Jan. 17, 1977.
17. Interview with Dr. Kubler-Ross in Feb. 1977, *Fate* Magazine. Used by special permission.

3

Rest in Peace?

Death has really changed. It has become very complicated. And as we try to arrive at a new definition of death that will satisfy the latest social concepts as well as the life-after-death reports, we run into quite a few problems.

It is central to our entire discussion in this book that we attempt to explain what death is *now*. We need to know if those people who tell of the next world really did die. And if they really have returned from the dead, we certainly want to know how we can all get in on this.

Samuel Johnson said, "The whole of life is but keeping away the thoughts of death." And that seemed true at the time. But nowadays a big part of some peoples' lives amounts to purposely thinking about death and wondering what it really involves. From the doctors, who must make an ever more cautious decision on just when people have really departed; to the life-after-death researchers, who are tackling a truly new area of life; to the mediums who say, "We told you so"; death has begun to present new vistas.

Our concern in this chapter is to define physiological death — the moment when the body, at least, has truly ceased to live. Then we will approach the broader questions of the philosophical and theological meanings of death.

Figuring out when the body has died is not as easy as it used to be.

IT'S GETTING HARD TO DIE

You can't just die these days in some situations. If you are about to slip off from, say, a heart attack or a respiratory failure, a skillful doctor can hang onto you interminably!

The term "cardiac arrest" is an interesting invention of our times. Not too long ago when your heart stopped you died, and that was a guarantee. There were no ifs, ands or buts about it when your heart stopped. That used to be the end of your case. You were as good as buried. You were "the late" so-and-so.

But as medical technology advanced doctors found ways to get your tired old engine started again. So now when your heart stops you are *not* dead; you are suffering a cardiac arrest. The implication is, of course, that your condition is temporary and, with immediate attention it can be alleviated.

Now all of us certainly applaud this advance in medical science, and truly, lives are being preserved daily. To the last one of us (assuming we don't consider death a good bargain in the light of the current findings) we are grateful. Should we have a heart attack we will be more than thankful for the new techniques.

But they have tended to make the definition of physical death just a bit more complicated.

30

In the old days when you stopped breathing your heirs would begin to divide your estate, and that's all there was to that. Your funeral arrangements started when your lungs stopped.

But nowadays when you stop breathing you are experiencing "cessation, of respiration." Your respiration may very well commence again in the presence of the right doctor with the right machine.

Again, we are grateful. We who want to go on living can't give thanks enough for a machine that breathes for us when we can't manage on our own.

But that definition of death keeps on getting more elusive.

We could go on and on describing conditions that used to seal our doom but which now yield to the remarkable resuscitation and mechanical life support procedures. Obviously, we can't just die, at least with the old meanings of death, the way things are.

The new systems of preserving life have created paradoxical situations. "Clinical death" is said to occur today in individuals who still function biologically. They are simultaneously dead and alive, depending on your definition. They breathe, eat and eliminate; their blood circulates healthfully; they may be comatose and beyond communication, but they still function in ways that living people function. They are usually damaged beyond repair, but are kept operative by machines.

Such was the case of Karen Ann Quinlan, whom we mentioned in the previous chapter. Miss Quinlan had mixed alcohol and drugs, apparently fatally, and her condition was grave. The resuscitation programs were equal to her disability however, and she lay out-of-touch but functioning on round-the-clock care in a hospital. There was no hope whatever for her ultimate recovery. She was merely being "preserved."

That she was not dead was provable by certain technical definitions, but for all practical purposes Karen was gone. Her parents sought to have the machines stopped so that their daughter might be allowed to rest at last.

And that, as is well known, got into quite a tangle. With no disrespect for either the Quinlans or the legal forces that struggled with her one-of-a-kind situation, the matter became so confused that the public became fed up with it all.

The plug was finally pulled but the answer to the dilemma was not found. When the machines were stopped, Miss Quinlan remained alive, or at least in the state she was in. And no one came up with any clear understanding of what that state should be called. Karen Quinlan lives, but where is she now?

Death has been defined recently in the courts as, "Not a continuing event...(but) an event that takes place at a precise time." Medical journals have it as, "A process and not a moment in time."[1]

Those two definitions diametrically disagree.

WHO IS DEAD?

Our first concern here is to unravel what death really is in order to know if the reports of "life after death" have any substance. We can certainly not undertake the morass of legal, technical and moral difficulties involved with mechanical life sustenance, but we *are* interested in knowing who was dead and who was not.

The first difficulty comes in qualifying exactly what sort of cases the experimenters like Drs. Moody and Kubler-Ross dealt with in their research. It is commonly reported in the press that those researchers dealt exclusively with people who had experienced "clinical death," but this is far from true. Many of the presented cases were not involved with certifiable death at all.

In Moody's research, which caused quite a stir, some two-thirds of his original cases were secondhand reports. It is difficult to trust the sort of testimony that goes, "I knew a man who said..." when dealing with so remarkable a subject as life after death. These were largely deleted from Moody's collection when it came time to publish and they do not appear in his book. The remaining 50 cases are divided into two major kinds: (1) *a close encounter* with death that may or may not involve some physical disability; (2) the "clinical death" experiences.

Now there is quite a difference between a subject who says, "I was about to drown and I glimpsed the other world, but then I was pulled out of the water," and a subject who "died" according to diagnostic machines in an emergency room. But Moody sees the two as making a sort of continuum; subjects who were sick or injured and certified dead were "more dead" than subjects who merely had a brush with death.

For our purposes we must know who was really *dead*, so to speak, and we must carefully consider the experiences of the "most dead" people who participated. Those who merely had a scare, it stands to reason, probably did not really enter some afterlife world.

HOW DEAD WERE YOU?

But it's kind of hard to ask people, "Well, just how dead *were* you?"

Actually, those who were certified dead by doctors or life-system measuring machines were not conscious and cannot say when they felt "dead." We all have visions when we lose consciousness every night — we call them dreams. Some are pleasant and others are scary. But we don't say that we entered another world, or another life, when we slept. A machine calibrating your life systems would measure you as "deadest" when you are sleeping, but you wouldn't dream of calling the visions you have an after-death glimpse into another existence.

So, just considering those who were certified dead by machine — were they really dead, and *how* dead?

There are still some problems here. Physicians, lawyers and laymen ultimately disagree as to the moment, or process, of death. David Henden, author of *Death As a Fact of Life*, carps, "The fact is that the specifics of determining death may even vary from one physician to the next."[2]

But in many cases it is a matter of life and death to diagnose death correctly. We would be most upset with the doctor who decided to transplant the heart of a loved one while that loved one lay seemingly dead, but in reality was still very much alive! Medical records are replete with cases of people in comas, with certain definitive signs of death registered by machine, simply waking up *after weeks or months* of "clinical death." Obviously, genuine death gets harder to determine in the presence of artificial mechanical-support systems, and books on euthanasia get more and more complicated.[3]

It is commonly held that resuscitation is impossible after five minutes without oxygen going to the brain. Irreversible brain damage is supposed to occur in that dire circumstance. But this five minutes has proved only an average figure. Dr. Moody has found cases "where resuscitation took place after twenty minutes with no evidence of brain damage."[4] Dr. Kubler-Ross refers to some patients supposedly dead up to *four hours* with no signs of brain damage or other disability which would normally accompany such critical conditions.[5] She touches on one case of a person "dead" twelve-and-a-half hours, and successfully resuscitated, but her report doesn't give the circumstances surrounding this record-breaking performance.[6] (That would certainly be time for a leisurely tour of the other world if that individual really took the trip.)

Both Moody and Kubler-Ross own up to the difficulties and shortcomings involved with this peculiar research. As to the best of cases — those who claim to have survived clinical death — Kubler-Ross asks:

How many are genuine? And then among the genuine, how many showed no vital signs and in the old days would have been considered dead, and how many would qualify according to present-day criteria of the definition of death, including cessation of brain-wave activity? To get scientifically valid cases is extremely difficult. [7]

And Dr. Moody admits:

What I've shown is not proof. I haven't collected a random sample or done a number of things that would make it "scientific." [8]

THREE GOOD WAYS TO DIE

To get down to the most reliable definitions of death, there are at least three medical conditions where most people would give you full credit for having died. Moody cites them all.

First of all, when your heart stops beating, your blood pressure is unreadable, your body temperature drops, etc. — when your vital functions utterly fail — it is generally agreed that you are dead. This clinical definition of death has been used for centuries by doctors and lay people alike.

The second "sure-death" condition is the total absence of brain wave activity. When your brain stops working you are gone, it is widely agreed.

Third — and this is the most complete definition, and the one we favor — you are considered dead when you suffer an *irreversible* loss of your vital functions.

Death must be defined as that state in which physical resuscitation is impossible.

Looking back at the first two definitions, we can see that they leave loopholes. People have been resuscitated from such critical conditions in recent times, strange as it seems.

With the first condition above, the "clinical death" condition, we must add the term "irreversible" to the failure of the vital signs. This is simply because what has appeared to be an utter failure of body functions can be reversed with the new machines. Blood pressure has gone off the scale, persuading attending doctors that the patient was deceased, only to reappear on the scale when the appropriate mechanical procedure was applied. Heart failure, respiratory failure, dilation of the pupils, decrease in body temperature — all these common signs of physiological death have at one time or another yielded resuscitation. The patients were apparently alive through it all.

For our purposes here, it is important to realize that our supposed "clinical death" cases come under that incomplete first definition. The people reporting "life after death" experiences tend to have been merely "clinically dead" in the best of cases, whereas they may never have died at all. Their condition was certified *before resuscitation*. They may have well been pronounced dead, but, since they are still with us, it seems reasonable to assume that they were *not* dead. They were critically disabled, but not beyond resuscitation.

The new clinical situations naturally raise much suspicion. Can I honestly call a vision I may have had during the period between my disability and my resuscitation a "life-after-death" experience? Was I really dead?

Author Hendon, quoted above, refers to the case of a soldier in Vietnam whose guard dog stepped on a land mine right beside him.[9] The mortally wounded soldier was brought to a field hospital with no pulse, no respiration and no heartbeat. Army doctors worked feverishly for 45 minutes on resuscitation — heart massage and artificial respiration — but the electrocardiograph showed no heart activity during their efforts. The doctors then diagnosed the patient as clinically dead and sent the body to Graves

Registration. The cadaver lay there for several hours awaiting embalming. When the embalmer was finally available the procedure was set up. But just as the embalmer was about to inject the fluid he noticed a pulse!

The soldier was taken back to the hospital and resuscitated again. He is alive and well today.

Clinical death doesn't always equal actual death.

We think the soldier never did die. We think he was misdiagnosed as dead. But if he'd had a dream, say, during his hours in Grave Registration, and if he had then been told that he'd been "brought back to life," we suppose he would regard his dream as an after-death experience. And there would be another one of those cases of "a look at the other side."

That's why we ask for that term, "irreversible." A definition of death cannot be accurate without it anymore.

As to the second definition of death — the absence of brain wave activity — there is an increasing trend to accept this condition as the valid indicator of death. But here again it is found that the condition can be unreliable as an indicator.

First, the electroencephalograph (EEG) machine is a complicated one, difficult to set up, especially in emergency situations. Even practiced professionals are predisposed to confusion and error in the face of impending death. Getting correct readings is difficult.

Secondly, there have been some cases where flat EEG tracings (indicating no brain activity whatever) were obtained in people who were later resuscitated. This situation tends to occur in cases involving very low body temperatures (e.g. during certain heart surgery and in drug overdose cases where the drugs act as a suppressant of the central nervous system.) Flat EEG readings in these cases have gone on for 24 hours in patients who then completely recovered![10]

Third, in cases where an after-death experience is related, there is no good way to tell if the patient had this experience during the flat reading time, or before or after it. I may have a terrifying dream as I am rushed to the hospital following an automobile accident. My condition may then deteriorate until my EEG reading goes completely flat. I may be pronounced dead after many hours of flat readings. And then, if I am resuscitated and told I was brought back from the dead, I may very well assume that my dream, which I experienced when I was very much alive, was a picture of where I was when I was "dead." Obviously, my having had some sort of vision sometime during my total experience after the accident does not add up to my having seen life after death. And just as obviously, my EEG reading diagnosing me as dead was unreliable. "Reports of my death have been greatly exaggerated," as Mark Twain observed.

Finally, there is little agreement on just how lengthy a flat reading is necessary to certify death. Different circumstances provide different lengths of time of the absence of brain wave activity. Henden notes:

> Thus, one could consider that after 5 minutes of a flat EEG reading, meaningful life is extinct. Some biologists accept a shorter time — as short as one minute — as proof of death, while others adhere to the 24 or 48 hour time limits.[11]

It gives one pause. Obviously we would all prefer a practitioner who opts for the longest time before writing us off. Horrible things can happen to people not quite dead. To avert real catastrophe, the National Academy of Medicine of France chose the 48-hour flat EEG reading for certifying death in the case of transplant donors.[12]

With that much uncertainty attending the technique of diagnosing death by electroencephalographic readings, we must discount this method for our purposes.

Moody flatly admits that by the *third* definition, the one with the "irreversible" qualifier, "...none of my cases would qualify, since they all involved resuscitation."[13] Notwithstanding, it still remains the best definition — it leaves no room for error. If Moody, Kubler-Ross, Matson, et al, have been talking with people who perhaps never were dead after all, their research may say very little about life-after-death experiences.

BUT WHERE *DID* THEY GO?

But the people report those weird experiences all the same, *and the experiences seem to coincide!* The remarkable similarity of these life-after-death testimonies argues for their veracity. And the patients themselves tell us the experience was not like a dream but something else altogether. We are not completely willing to believe that every subject of these inquiries was really dead, due to our foregoing analyses of the definitions of death, but where *did* they all go? How did they happen to come up with such similar reports? Why do they all think they saw the "other side?"

Perhaps these folks *began* to die, and thus saw a glimpse of life after death. Perhaps, as some think, they would have gone on into that other life — the life after death — if the doctors hadn't intervened with their machines. This is the feeling we get from many of the testimonies.

But what are we really dealing with here?

We have some ideas — perhaps shocking ideas — that might lend an answer. But first we should more deeply analyze the life-after-death testimonies with a view to ferreting out their true characteristics.

Don't read the next chapter in the middle of the night.

1. David Hendin, *Death As a Fact of Life*, (New York: Warner) 1974, p. 24, cf 15-43, and *America*, September 27, 1975 quoting Dr. P. H. Muller in *The World Medical Journal*.
2. Hendin, p. 39.
3. John A. Behnke and Sissela Bok (eds.), *The Dilemma of*

    Euthanasia (Garden City, New York: Anchor Press/Double-
day) Appendix 3; Henden, Chapter 1.
4. Moody, *Life After Life*, p. 101.
5. Interview in Feb. 1977, *Fate* Magazine, p. 68-9. Used by
special permission.
6. *Reader's Digest*, August 1976, p. 84.
7. Interview in Feb. 1977, *Fate* Magazine, p. 68-9. Used by
special permission
8. *National Observer*, May 15, 1976, p. 10.
9. Henden, p. 39-40.
10. Ibid., p. 29, 32.
11. Ibid., p. 28-9.
12. Ibid.
13. Moody, p. 103.

4

Death—
The Guided Tour

The people who have reportedly come back from the dead have a lot in common. They have at least seemed to take very similar tours of the next world, and there are details about their experiences and personalities that agree from case to case.

Dr. Moody's set of criteria seem to repeat reliably throughout the reports of his subjects, but it might also be said that the subjects normally cite goings-on that have always been hallmarks of fictional or mediumistic after-death experiences.

Some of Moody's criteria will be immediately recognized by those who have heard· of after-death experiences in some other connection. The idea of the subject traveling somewhere out of the body, strange sounds, the sensation of going down a long dark tunnel, the recognition of some line or border between life and death, the encountering of a "Being of Light"—these are almost classic features of where we will all supposedly go on that last trip. Psychic literature and horror movies both ring with such phenomena.

But it is interesting that the criteria also hold up between researchers. Working independently Drs. Kubler-Ross, Karlis Osis and several others seem to have come up with much the same data. The criteria does seem representative of the experiences. Kubler-Ross, in an interview, eloquently and very positively described this feeling of a common trend in after-death experiences:

> The universal common denominator for all the patients we have interviewed is that they have this beautiful feeling of peace. Sometimes there is music, but the most common feeling is of peace — no pain, no fear, no anguish. And wholeness. People who are blind can see and people who have had leg amputations can walk.

> The next phenomenon is that they are greeted by someone who has died before them. They float away, usually physically out of the room or away from the accident scene, away from where the death occurred. They are greeted by an important next of kin...

> None of these patients will ever again be afraid to die. That's another common denominator. The experience really changes the quality of life...Their whole value system changes.[1]

Our own research indicates that there are also serious discrepancies between cases and that not every experience is that positive. Studying great numbers of cases from the literature and from our own research, we found our own set of criteria for these experiences, which did not differ greatly from the Moody or Kubler-Ross criteria, but which suggests quite different conclusions.

We're not quite sold on the idea that what those people saw is what we all will get.

THE LIGHT AT THE END OF THE TUNNEL

We're very interested in that light, or "Being of Light," that many of those people saw. It seems that almost everyone who had a life-after-death experience saw the light.

This is one of the most prevalent and important factors to us. The light is unquestionably a comforting thing. Sometimes it is just a diffused glow and sometimes it is a being that "walks and talks." Sometimes the light takes the dead one on a tour of the new surroundings, brief but seemingly meant to provide confidence and peace.

Oftentimes, as in several of the Moody cases, the light discusses a situation from the life of the newly deceased one and invariably reassures the understandably troubled party that all is well. It seems that complete approval awaits all of us on the other side according to what the being of light has disclosed in a great many instances.

Sometimes the patient interprets the light as a religious personality. The light can be God Himself, Krishna, an angel or Jesus Christ, biblically "The light of the world." Dr. George Ritchie's experience is very representative:

> I was told to stand up. My own spiritual body was standing up from the floor beside my physical body lying in the bed. Someone was lying on the bed I had just left.
>
> Christ appeared as an extremely bright light. The room was illuminated with brilliance, and it was a presence so comforting and joyous that I wanted to lose myself forever in the wonder of it. [2]

Dr. Ritchie discussed matters of gravity with "Christ" on that occasion:

The first question Christ put to me was: "What have you done with your life that you can show me?" Then I realized what He meant by that.

Dr. Ritchie underwent the "review" of his life:

It was a panoramic view of my life for Him and I both to see. And He was asking me if I could accept my fellow human beings the way He knew all about me and accepted me and loved me; not what religion I had or what I said, but how I actually lived and loved with my fellow human beings.

The subject then enjoyed the brief tour. He reports only:

Then He conducted me through different realms.

This subject reaches a profound conclusion from his presumably inexplicable trip through the "realms:"

I now believe that life is a continuent. What we learn here does not go to waste, but continues as a learning process.

These realms were basically to guide us and are similar to the realm in which you and I live. They demonstrate the cause and effect of that which we bring upon ourselves. [3]

Dr. Ritchie reported his unique experience, an unusually complete and relevant understanding of the next world, at a 1970 meeting of the Spiritual Frontiers Fellowship. [4] SFF is a group that seeks to integrate Christianity and parapsychology. It was founded by the medium Arthur Ford, who contacted "the dead" with ease for occult-minded clients.

Mediumism and psychic powers are the concern of the SFF and they feel that the biblical admonitions against such inquiries no longer apply today.[5]

Searching through cases too numerous to detail here, the authors found that the Being of Light emanates definite characteristics. Rather like the "spirit guides" of mediums, the Being of Light is non-condemning and provides feelings of warmth, peace, love and joy. The Being prefers to speak in religious and moral terms, has great wisdom and is wonderfully reassuring to his clients. He is understanding, forgiving and even has a sense of humor. Dr. Moody, relating the experiences of his patients with the Being of Light, is encouraging:

> They found, much to their amazement, that even when their most apparently awful and sinful deeds were made manifest before the Being of Light, the Being responded not with anger and rage, but rather only with understanding, and even with humor.[6]

It told them that even in their sins, they were learning, progressing.

We would all suppose from this that we're in much better shape than we thought. Even those who deeply respect the commandments of Christ against sin in the scriptures can relax, according to these reports. Christ has apparently foregone His former aversion to our "awful and sinful deeds" and we can rest assured that we're actually doing very well in our lives. If we are to believe these reports, death is a wonderful place.

Again, the Being of Light is not always interpreted as Christ. He has been simply "a spirit" to some people, "a saint" like Peter or Paul to others, and on through an infinite number of identities seemingly associated with whomever the dead one would prefer to meet over there.

But whoever he is, he's very easy to like.

45

That "review of life" undergone by Ritchie and so many others is also a fascinating concept, and one that has been assumed since the times of the ancients. Since man does understand good and evil, he has tended to picture himself as earning some grade or score in this life. When life is over it will be time for the final exam and all deeds done on earth will be reviewed. Rewards and punishments presumably await all men.

This is thoroughly biblical as well as historical, as we shall see, and it seems logical that folks coming back from the dead would see a glimpse of the process. But it never seems to bother anyone and the part about rewards and punishments is not usually included in the typical after-death experience. The individual seems only to undergo a passive review of his life's events, sometimes down to the smallest detail, and to re-experience the emotions that accompanied all those events.

The review is somehow a "quickie," lasting only an instant but being at the same time very thorough. Such are things in the next world.

The Being of Light doesn't seem overly concerned with the review, sometimes not even being present but other times acting as a sort of neutral director of the exercise. The Being apparently prefers the role of an impartial observer during the review, usually wrapping things up with some advice for the subject on learning to love more and gathering more knowledge when he returns to life.

This obvious philosophy about love and knowledge is very typical of the literature of the occult, where spirit guides are forever advising their mediums in the same manner. Love and worldly knowledge are icons of all religions and one might have hoped for something more significant from the Being of Light.

Visiting one's dead relatives and friends seems a lot more acceptable than an interview with the Being of Light, and people invariably enjoy it. Matson gives a definitive case of a man's *two* deaths, reported by his pleased wife:

> He was not the same man (when he came back to life). He had died and gone to the next life where he was met by many of his loved ones who had passed over before him ...All during the war there was nobody in Norfolk in such demand to talk with parents who had lost their sons. He could bring real comfort because he knew what their boys were facing in the next life. He had been there. [7]

Here was a man with a mission! People took very seriously his trip into the beyond and were comforted by his positive impressions. To his wife he was "not the same man" because he had a new sense of usefulness to his neighbors, having seen that gratifying place where their loved ones now resided.

This subject lived on for some time. When he finally died permanently, his wife was on the scene and gave this report:

> Aubrey was in two worlds at the same time. He was not only aware of me and talking to me, but he greeted by name some thirty or forty friends and relatives who were waiting for him... [8]

The role of the dead, much of the time, is apparently to ease the transition into the next world for the newcomer. Obviously, when friends and relatives are involved that harrowing experience is that much easier. But they are not always involved, of course.

Kubler-Ross says that invariably a loved one who has died previously is the key figure in easing the subject across the threshold of death,[9] but Moody's research indicates a greater variety of personalities in the beyond. The research by parapsychologist Osis in the U.S. indicates that a very high proportion of those who met personalities in the next world found close relatives (83%).[10]

Again we strike that familiar chord with mediumistic and psychic experiences. Some other-worldly personalities are friendly but some are "unknown spirits." They both tend to tell the newcomer to go back into life again, reportedly.

Apparently, as with the Being of Light, there's no telling ahead of time who one may meet over there. The Being of Light may be any number of personalities, though usually a being familiar to the subject. In just the same way, the spirits over there may be unknown to the subject or they may more often be family members.

You can't make reservations and you can't tell who you'll meet when you get there.

MORE PROBLEMS

Among the other criteria of these experiences which we have selected are loneliness, a sense of great beauty and a cultic feel surrounding the whole enterprise.

The loneliness happens because the subject is out of touch with this world yet still seems to remain at least partially in it. When an individual travels out of his body, as many report they did, he can see and hear the things in this world, but he cannot communicate with the living.

Many report the frustrating experience of floating up to the ceiling of a hospital room, or hovering above the scene of an accident they experienced, and watching helplessly as people worked over their own

48

bodies. They wanted to say — especially to stricken loved ones — "I'm perfectly okay! I feel good! Please don't cry!" But that was impossible.

The loneliness was alleviated for many when the spirits showed up, but we suppose that depended on just who the spirits *were*. The relatives in the beyond would be sympathetic, with their mission being to facilitate the transition. The Being of Light is invariably most tactful and accommodating. But the unknown spirits would probably offer less comfort to one newly dead and still looking back, we imagine.

At the moment when the subject is out of his body he seems to have a spiritual body, which has no effect on this world. Sometimes he doesn't experience having a body at all — he is just a concentration of energy, but in any case he is out of touch, and feeling it. Few experience the re-entry into their physical bodies when they return from the dead. They are usually not conscious at that point. Presumably they come back as the result of an extraordinary medical procedure — electric shock or adrenalin applied directly to the heart, for example — but they are not as aware of the return trip as they were of leaving the body.

As to the sense of great beauty which many subjects report, this is an outstandingly positive part of the after-death experience. It's not just that there is beautiful scenery in the next world, which apparently there is, but that an all-pervading feeling of loveliness accompanies the whole manifestation. Sometimes exquisite music is part of the overall beauty of the setting.

Many do not want to return to this life and some people became most upset about being "brought back." They would gladly have stayed to see more of that stunning beauty.

The experience seems to remain with the resuscitated subject so that his life is changed and his anxieties about death greatly assuaged. There is no longer any doubt about life after death in the subject's mind and he looks forward to a future, permanent residence in the other world. He wants to tell others about it and may feel that he has a mission to spread the word about the joy of dying. Mediums who consult the dead also display this sense of mission, encouraging people to think positively about the beyond and to regard death as a step upwards.

The cultic feel to the experiences is evidenced in the fact that they tend to happen to those who have little biblical comprehension of life and death. We shall go deeply into what the Bible has to say on this vital matter; since it is unquestionably the world's best-seller on the subject of life after death, but suffice it here to say that there are very few born again believers coming forward with these experiences. And we would expect otherwise, considering the fact that Bible-reading people firmly *believe* in life after death. We would think that most of the testimony about the great beauty, the Being of light and the other positive criteria associated with these experiences would come from those who count on heaven when they die.

Those who believe in God, as He is expressed in the scriptures, sometimes recognize and even praise the idea of the light, the gorgeous music, the attending angels, and so forth, reported by those who have died. But surprisingly, those who have died are not necessarily among those who would biblically be awaiting those very experiences.

On the other hand, the experiences seem to come from those who hold non-biblical views of life and death (Gilmore bet his very life on his convictions about reincarnation.) What is called "astral projection" in the world of the occult is identified as something like out-of-the-body travel in the world of life after death. The characteristics of the two are very hard to separate actually.

Of course, there are many people of *professed* belief involved with these reports (nominal Christians), but we would have expected a large number of biblically

50

oriented folks to say, "I saw just what I expected to see from my study of the Bible." But no one has given such a testimony through the volumes of reported cases.

There are ministers involved with these cases, but as we saw they are also often involved in such biblically prohibited exercises as psychic research or mediumistic practices. They would not represent Christianity to true Christians, though they may well profess to have actually seen Jesus Christ. In Dr. Ritchie's report where the Being of Light appeared to be Christ, we found the Savior taking a totally opposite position to His own teaching in the biblical record, stating it did not matter what religion a person belonged to.[11]

People who die and come back do not give us any biblical heaven-or-hell picture of things over there. There may be, however, a "city of light" which occultists refer to from their "astral" travels. The situation seems to never be so positive as to have someone saying they'd been to the true heaven and never so negative that they say they'd seen hell. However, there are two disturbing cases in the Osis research where the doctor reports:

> The patient had a horrified expression, turned his head in all directions and said, "Hell, Hell, all I see is Hell." Another had the terrifying feeling of being buried alive.[12]

But in general, death has a very good press. These negative cases are by far the exception.

The after-death experience cuts across cultures, religious beliefs (except biblical belief) and nations. One can find these stories in any nation of the world and they match up fairly well, the majority being positive.

We should note, before leaving our section on problems in this experience, that it is not at all wise to assume from the research so far available that the life-after-death experience is an entirely fine thing. Despite the highly positive reports, there is reason to think that there is an underlying negative quality to this entire matter.

Dr. John Garfield of the University of California, who has done extensive research into the life-after-death experience, cautioned interviewers:

> I hope you won't print that everyone who dies has a glorious, mystical experience. It's very easy to read those books (Moody and Kubler-Ross) and come to the conclusion that everyone has a glorious experience.[13]

DON'T THROW THIS BOOK AWAY YET!

Now we're coming to the best part of this book.

Up to now we have tried to furnish an impartial survey of the life-after-death experiences. Now we will move on to analyzing what's really going on.

What are these experiences? Why are they happening? What do they have to do with *you*?

How is it that people are returning from the dead with reports of the other world these days? Were they really dead or were they just dreaming? Are things as they say over there or are we being kidded? Should we worry about dying or should we look forward to it? Should we necessarily try to live honorably and rightly or, in view of the reportedly relaxed standards of the next world, shall we accommodate all of our desires and explain later?

Note that there are many *conceivable* possibilities. Perhaps there is a natural trigger mechanism (e.g., extreme physiological stress and anesthesia have been known to cause out of the body sensations). Perhaps some stories are fabrications or misinterpretations of something else. Perhaps they are all in the mind. One of the most logical possibilities is that which we present in the next chapter, and it is in this area we will concentrate.

A much-quoted libertine once raised his glass and sang, "Eat, drink and be merry, for tomorrow we die!" It gives us all a bittersweet feeling. But we can now make it, "Eat, drink and be merry, for tomorrow we *live again*?"

Read on.

1. Interview reported in Feb. 1977. *Fate* Magazine, p. 10. Used by special permission.
2. Interview by The World News Corp., 730 3rd Ave., New York City, N.Y. 10017. From *The Star* Magazine, January 11, 1977.
3. Ibid.
4. Archie Matson, *Afterlife*, (New York: Harper and Row) 1977, p. 32.
5. "Spiritual Frontiers Fellowship—Its Principles, Purposes and Program;" *The Biblical Prohibition in Deuteronomy* by J. MacDonald; *The Church and Psychical Research* by J. D. Pearse—Higgens, available from S.F.F.
6. Moody, *Life After Life*, p. 70.
7. Matson, p. 18-9.
8. Ibid.
9. *Los Angeles Times*, July 1, 1976.
10. Karlis Osis, *Deathbed Observations by Physicians and Nurses* (New York: Parapsychology Foundation) Monograph No. 3, p. 68-9.
11. See Dr. Ritchie's comments in the Washington Post, June 3, 1977.
12. Osis, p. 30.
13. *Pageant Magazine*, February, 1977.

"There is no separate, indivisible, specific point of death. Life is a state of becoming, and death is a part of this process of becoming."

"Seth," the spirit entity speaking through medium, Jane Roberts, *Seth Speaks*, p. 138

"Death is the final stage of growth in this life. There is no total death."

Elizabeth Kubler-Ross, *Death: The Final Stage of Growth*, p. 166

"You surely shall not die."

The Serpent, Genesis 3:4 NAS

5

Spiritual Warfare

The Bible indicates that all mankind is caught in the midst of a battle of supreme magnitude.

We war against "principalities and powers," to quote the apostle Paul. Like the beleaguered Job, we are all the objects of spiritual warfare.

A lot of people won't like this chapter because it will tread upon their material views of life. We find it necessary, due to our subject, to talk about spiritual things, and spiritual things upset people. Although most of the American public believes implicitly in horoscopes; swallows whole movies like "The Exorcist" and "The Omen;" privately consults mediums and "reader-advisors" about stock market purchases or love affairs; buys millions of Ouija boards, Tarot cards and the like; utilizes the services of clairvoyants to find criminals or lost keys; supports parapsychological research, which attempts to make a scientific study of the supernatural; pursues occult religion in endless forms; it is still considered somehow unsophisticated to believe in the world of the supernatural.

We are behind the scenes, a very supernatural-believing society, but when the answer to some real-life dilemma falls into this category it is very unpopular. Be that as it may, we find these stories of life after death highly supernatural in kind. We find that it is absolutely necessary to refer to this "nether world" of things to explain what's going on.

The occult world is fully operative all around us, it should surprise no one to know. A staggering amount of people are steadily involved in everything from psychic research to out-and-out Satan worship as part of our open-minded way of doing things lately. Cults flourish, appearing overnight and gathering thousands of adherents with promises of the "Divine Light," peace through meditation of some sort, or the soon coming of some Aquarian age of full-time fun and kicks.

We find that these life-after-death stories — particularly the good reputation of death as we are now coming to see it — is something like positive public relations for this entire occult movement. We suspect that something much bigger than the innocent folks who tell of these experiences and the doctors who publicize them is behind all of this. Strange as our theory may seem, we think we can offer some compelling evidence to the open-minded reader.

SCIENCE CARRIES THE BALL

We have come to think that when *science* approves of something it's got to be good for us. *Science* is today's ultimate endorser of products and ideas.

When soap companies supposedly find a more effective ingredient for their product they don't take the credit for it. They announce instead, *Science has discovered B-33!* When we need clothing we are urged to take advantage of *miracle* fibers newly discovered by *science*. Even love problems can be solved when an understanding computer fixes you up with the perfect mate, *scientifically*.

We certainly respect science. We utilize scientific procedures in our own research. But we have seen, and so has everyone else, science perverted by a philosophy or doctrine. In the USSR science tends to discover what the Communist Party has prescribed to be profitable science. In this nation, science is invoked to hawk goods, prove political theories, regulate the economy and testify to temporary insanity in murder trials. Thinking people are growing tired of science that is not truly science pronouncing upon a whole world of emotional issues and unscientific matters.

Lately, science has gone into the occult world and has lent its powerful endorsement to some of the most surprising inquiries. Would you believe that science now tends to support the conclusions of mediums who consult the dead? Sample the following statement of parapsychologist Osis, a key researcher of life after death phenomena in America and also India:

> This research certainly does not cinch the answer to the problem of survival after death. It's not definitely proven like you can prove a geometry problem. But it does show that the information from the dying is consistent across culture with the idea of life after death.
>
> It also does something else. Previously in parapsychology, the emphasis was on what mediums had to say. Here we had a chance to look at the same problem through the eyes of the dying in two widely divergent cultures. This gives us a better idea of what might be there, and *it also tends to confirm much of the picture gained through mediumship*.[1] (Our emphasis).

That gives some idea of what we mean by science that is not science. We think proving a geometry problem is science. We respectfully think that

57

testimonies of *dying* people about life *after death* do not confirm *anything*, least of all what mediums have to tell us. We think we're reading someone's philosophy when we read a passage like that above, not a scientific report.

But it is clear that a statement like that one is taken by most of the people who read it as some kind of scientific endorsement — maybe not terribly definite, but part of science anyway. And that's where the public relations come in. Science is now being used as a sales tool, not just for marketing products, but also for supporting ideas. And we think some of the ideas scientists choose to support are very bad ideas.

Dr. Osis and the others have now progressed to where they think science has verified something purely supernatural or occult. They no longer need to offer the testimonies of mediums, which most of us reject out of hand — they can now offer "scientific" testimony. The afterlife is now becoming a scientific phenomena, presumably measurable and capable of replicable experiments. Presently, we suppose, science will tell us where and when to die, and what to say when we get there. That's the way things seem to be going.

It's not really a case of scientists trying to perpetrate evil on the rest of us. Rather, it is the basic pride of mankind at work. Men refuse to be outsmarted by anyone, or any force in this universe. We are never deceived; we figure out everything. We are in control and there is no unseen influence upon us. We know everything about life and death, or we are at least coming to that knowledge, and we don't need "principalities and powers," God or the devil, as part of our theories.

This situation was predicted brilliantly by the novelist C. S. Lewis in *The Screwtape Letters*. The elder devil Screwtape is philosophizing to his nephew Wormwood about the best battle tactic for getting men to follow the devil:

I have great hopes that we shall learn in due time how to emotionalize and mythologize their science to such an extent that what is, in effect, a belief in us will creep in while the human mind remains closed to belief in the Enemy. [2]

THE "RESURRECTION" OF ARTHUR FORD

The "resurrection" of Arthur Ford goes back a few years, not being part of the new wave of interesting cases, but it is one of the best by far. Seldom has anyone reported so complete an afterlife experience.

Ford was critically ill. In a few moments he would die. "Give him the needle, he may as well be comfortable," the doctor told the nurse. But even though he should have stayed dead, the man came back, having been in a coma for two weeks. During his "death," he was told he had a mission to accomplish, and hence he was being returned. In his own words, he records his "death":

> Next, I was floating in the air above my bed. I could see my body, but had no interest in it. There was a feeling of peace, a sense that all was well...I found myself floating through space, without effort...
>
> Now, there appeared a green valley with mountains on all sides, illuminated everywhere by a brilliance of light and color impossible to describe. People were coming toward me from all around, people I had known and thought of as "dead." I knew them all. Many I had not thought of for years, but it seemed that everyone I had ever cared about was there to greet me...
>
> At some point...I found myself...in an enormous anteroom. They said I was to remain

there until some sort of disposition had been made of my case...Guiltily, I began an inventory of my life. It did not make a pretty picture. The people at the long tables were also reviewing the record, but the things that worried me did not seem to have much interest for them. The conventional sins I was warned about as a child were hardly mentioned...The "Judges"...mentioned my having failed to accomplish "what they knew I had to finish." There was a purpose for me, it seemed, and I had not fulfilled it. There was a plan for my life and I had misread the blueprint. 'They're going to send me back,' I thought, and I didn't like it...

When I was told I had to return to my body, I fought having to get back into that beaten, diseased hulk I had left behind...I was standing before a door. I knew if I passed through it, I would be back where I had been. I decided I wouldn't go. Like a spoiled child in a tantrum, I pushed my feet against the wall and fought. There was a sudden sense of hurtling through space. I opened my eyes and looked into the face of a nurse.[3]

A truly classic case!

Arthur Ford's experience really covers all bases. If one refers to the Moody criteria, he covers almost all of them. He is representative of the criteria of the other researchers as well, and he certainly has a great deal to offer by way of our own criteria for these experiences.

The interesting part is what became of the resurrected Ford, and here we begin our solution to the mystery of these experiences.

Arthur Ford was one of the world's most renown trance mediums. It was he who persuaded Bishop Pike into his strange voyages to the world of the dead. He was the founder of the anti-biblical Spiritual Frontiers Fellowship. His books, his remarkable seances, his 40 years of occult activities on four continents witnessed on television by millions, his highly celebrated impact on Pike, his hatred of biblical doctrine and his articulate good works for the cause of the occult all constitute one of the most profoundly effective campaigns in the spiritual warfare of the present century.

Ford cannot be given credit enough for his total commitment to white-washing death itself:

> I know that great opportunities await us where we are all going. I hope when the time comes, I will have completed that earth task for which I believe my life in the earth sphere was fashioned: to use whatever special talents were given me, through no merit of mine, to remove for all time the fear of the death passage from earth minds....[4]

Now, that's encouraging. Talk about "Rest in peace!" Ford has almost no peer among those who market a highly salable occult product.

Ford's concept of a "mission" that he is to accomplish is a popular one among occultists. Some people "back from the dead" feel inspired to share their experiences widely, with a view to calming folks about the consequences of dying. Death is a good thing, after all, and there is nothing to worry about, they preach.

. And, most emphatically, there will be no debts to pay upon death. The life led by the individual is of no importance—everybody gets a good reception on the other side.

That's the "gospel" — the "good news" — spread by Ford and many of his associates about death.

Another example of occult parallels is the book *Glimpses of the Beyond* by European parapsychologist, Jean-Baptiste Delacour. Detailing numerous near- and clinical-death experiences, the overall conclusion of the book is stated on the cover jacket:

> Perhaps the most arresting aspect of these accounts is that they agree so strongly with what many parapsychologists, using varying methods of investigation, have said about life after death. Delacour's subjects, who overcame a strange reluctance to talk about their experiences, present evidence that there is a hereafter, that our souls *do* live on, that we *will* encounter the souls of dead friends and relatives, and that we will be subsequently reincarnated. As a result, almost everyone who has undergone this experience has completely lost his fear of death.

Here again, we have the common occult elements — contact with the dead, reincarnation, and loss of the fear of death.

THE DEVIL MAKES THEM DO IT

When we say there are supernatural forces influencing the lives of human beings, we usually get laughs. Somehow the very people who consult the clairvoyants, hire Indians to do snow dances to encourage the spirits to rejuvenate the ski slopes of Colorado, and carefully check out the daily horoscopes are the first to laugh.

The idea of an active devil, right out of the pages of the Bible, is probably the biggest laugh-getter of all. When we say that it might well be the devil's plan to white-wash death itself we have people rolling in the aisles. If we say there is logic to the idea that Satan's plan would include a pleasant, no-responsibility death for everyone, we are thought to be religious fanatics.

Well and good. We'll own up to all that. We think there is a devil, there is demon activity, and these things have everything to do with this new rash of life-after-death reports.

Spiritual warfare is like any other kind of warfare.

Deception is an effective tactic. The devil knows better than to say, "God is a liar;" instead he says, "Everything God says is not necessarily true."

The Bible says one thing and the life-after-death people say another. God has described death — it's gravity and consequences — but people who've supposedly been there say it's not quite as God says it is.

It would be beyond our scope here to undertake a proof of the validity of the Bible. There are adequate books on that subject available everywhere, and even people with purely secular hearts are beginning to give the scriptures their due these days.[5] But when a biblical issue is attacked — especially an issue as vital as life and death — we feel we must join that particular battle. Martin Luther says:

> If I profess with the loudest voice and clearest exposition every portion of the truth of God except precisely that little point which the world and the Devil are at the moment attacking, I am not confessing Christ, however boldly I may be professing Christ. Where the battle rages, there the loyalty of the soldier is proved, and to be steady on the battlefield besides is merely flight and disgrace if he flinches at that point.

Evidences of demon activity are replete in the Bible, from Genesis to Revelation. Jesus Christ believed in and combatted demons, and those looking on in those electrifying gospel scenes never scoffed.

It is the nature and the task of demons, and their master, the devil, to undercut and counterfeit what God has established, be it religious faith, the sin concept or death itself. We can fully expect that if there is a way to relax people away from a natural fear of death, the enemy will find it and use it. If there is a way to convince people that sin in this life is of no consequence and that all will be forgiven in the next world, we can be sure that the negative forces in this spiritual battle will really work at it.

And we think that's what's going on.

The biblical explanation of death is very clear. It is final; it is deeply consequential. Each man dies once, with one of two possible results. Either the individual is forgiven and taken to be with God or he is not forgiven and is taken to the future home of the devil. That's putting it very simply but that's the fact of it, biblically.

The clinical death cases, however, present middle-ground alternatives and completely different pictures of how things are after death. The benevolence of the Being of Light, the music, the beautiful scenery and all the rest smack of that oldest of old-time religions, occult worship.

With the occultists everything is happiness. There is no need for salvation of any sort in this life because death provides no negative consequences. Mediums, consulting the other world, invariably find that all is well, and clinically resuscitated folks concur. Arthur Ford was truly a missionary, bringing reassuring news to those who are alive that we shall all profit greatly by dying, and he seems to have plenty of company.

Behind every occult phenomenon in the Bible stands the "father of all lies," as Jesus referred to him — the devil. From that first appearance of the serpent in the Garden of Eden, with his offer of new knowledge, to the coming antichrist of prophecy, Satan has always been and will always be at his post. The argument of the principalities and powers over the fate of Job is not finished yet. Each of us must finally say, "I trust in God," or "I don't," before the spiritual warfare is done.

THAT SAME OLD SONG AND DANCE

It seems that the clinical death experiences fit very well into the old, old story of occultic experiences. Matson goes so far as to say that "Mediumship is the crown which gives confirmation and clarity" to the deathbed experiences.[6] He reports on the research of Dr. Robert Crookall who "analyzed thousands of psychic experiences and (spirit) communications annd discovered that they form a pattern largely in conformity with the evidence presented (in Matson's reports on life-after-death cases)."[7]

In the analyses of coauthor Weldon the same similarities emerged. The works and views of such famous mediums and psychics as Ena Twigg, Ruth Montgomery, Jane Roberts, Tom Johanson, Irene Hughes, Ann Gehman, Carolyn Rosseter, and on and on, are replete with life-after-death experiences extremely similar to the new clinical death experiences, but achieved by means of spirit contact, astral projection and the like.[8] The cases seem almost interchangeable, with the reports from the hospital rooms being nearly identical with the reports from the seances.

The mediums, without exception, see the dead as being out there to help us — the beautiful landscapes, music and colors are all in their expected places. Psychic Hughes rhapsodizes:

> No one dies alone. Everyone is met on the other side by someone who cares...(In the other world) I felt great joy and delight...I wanted to stay forever. The other side is full of love and understanding and forgiveness...I have spoken to thousands of spirits and not one has said they are unhappy.

Medium Rosseter is reassuring:

> Passing over is a beautiful experience...We actually see our loved ones and recognize them. There is great joy at the reunion...No one sits in judgment.

The reader should note that we have changed bodies of literature for the above reports. The extremely similar testimonies in the earlier chapters were from scientifically reported clinical death cases, and these present reports are from interviews with psychics. The testimonies are so identical that there might be some confusion as to the sources, and that, of course, is our point.

We think the ultimate source — demon activity — is indeed the same.

Weldon's conclusions on the research into occult sources reveal three reliable observations:

1. The recent experiences detailed by researchers Moody, Kubler-Ross, Wheeler, Matson and the others parallel exactly those reported in the occult writings. Books reportedly written in a trance state, dictated from the spirit world, say essentially the same things about death that the "scientific" experiences portray. The occult view of death is exactly the same as the clinical view.

2. The occult writings are, without exception, anti-biblical. Often an entire book is produced through a medium by a controlling spirit and the book apparently represents the thoughts of that spirit. Many times the matters discussed are religious in nature, dealing with God and reflecting a moralistic view, but are never biblically accurate.

3. The people working in the occult areas of the psychic realm, parapsychology or religious occultism very often come out with a distinctly non-biblical view of God, salvation and the afterlife. Documentation by Drs. Koch, Montgomery and others detail a higher rate of insanity, suicide and demon possession among these persons. Occultic involvement is extremely dangerous.

4 Many of those who research the field of clinical death phenomena tend to end up involved in the occult[9] (See note for examples.)

Dr. John Montgomery warns against occult involvement in no uncertain terms:

> The tragedy of most sorcery, invocation of demons and related practices is that those who carry on these activities refuse to face the fact that they always turn out for the worst. What is received through the Faustian past never satisfies and one pays with one's soul in the end anyway.[10]

Dr. Kurt Koch, a biblical theologian who has counseled over 20,000 people, many of those in occult bondage, and has for some 40 years studied about the devil, analyzes the enemy of God with open eyes:

> "The devil is a many-sided and versatile demagogue. To the psychologist he says, 'I will give you new knowledge and understanding.' To the occultist he will say, 'I will give you the keys to the last secrets of creation.' He confronts the religionist and the moralist with a mask of integrity and promises them the very help of heaven. And finally to the rationalist and the liberalist he says, 'I am not there. I do not even exist.'

> The devil is a skillful strategist. He is the master of every tactic of the battlefield. He befogs the front. He hides behind a camouflage of empty religious talk. He operates through the use of the latest scientific method. He successfully fires and launches his arguments on the social and humane plane. And his sole aim is to deceive, to entice and to ensnare his victims." [11]

Of course, it's not fashionable to give the devil credit today for anything that's going on. "I am not there. I do not even exist," has been his best ploy lately.

IN THE INTERESTS OF SCIENCE?

Now the reader may well object and say, "Okay, suppose the devil does exist and suppose he's up to all of his old tricks. We're still getting our information from *scientists*, not mediums and psychics. Aren't the researchers who are honestly digging into this life-after-death question trustworthy? Don't they utilize the scientific method, which only seeks to discover what is true in an unbiased way? Don't they rely on

67

unimpeachable scientific sources for their data? Aren't they themselves merely unprejudiced inquirers into a new area?''

We wish they were. But the fact is, certain evidences suggest that such researchers as Kubler-Ross and Moody are not unbiased at all toward the occult world. Their activities, the research materials they utilize and their own personal biases suggest a less than scientifically pure approach to this arcane subject.

The *Yoga Journal* of September-October, 1976 enthusiastically reported the appearance of Dr. Kubler-Ross as a speaker at a holistic health conference in Sept., 1976.[12] (Holistic medicine often seeks to integrate occult healing techniques into medical practice — including psychic healing, consciousness exploration and the like![3]) Yoga adept Lennie Kronisch, R. N., director of the Holistic Health Institute of San Francisco, reported part of the Kubler-Ross lecture, and the profound impact it had on the *2300* attending M.D.'s, nurses and other medical professionals:

> ''Then visibly moved and emanating a glow of awe and wonder, she shared with us a profound mystical experience that had happened to her only the night before in the midst of a group of seventy-five people. She prefaced her narrative with the remark that only a short time ago she would not have found it possible to speak these words at a public forum. 'Last night, I was visited by Salem, my spirit guide, and two of his companions, Anka and Willie. They were with us until three o'clock in the morning. We talked, laughed and sang together. They spoke and touched me with the most incredible love and tenderness imaginable. This was the high-light of my life'. . .It was totally apparent to me that this beautiful experience had occurred when and how it did, so that it would be heard with this assemblage....

"As she concluded, there was a momentary silence and then the mass of people rose as one in tribute. Most of the audience, largely physicians and other health care professionals, was seemingly moved to tears. Many left the room, deeply affected and unable to give their attention to the rest of the program."[14]

Kubler-Ross further shows her occultic leanings in the following quotation:

"From my interviews with the dying and with mediums, I would describe the other world as similar to ours...We will be met by the ones we loved the most in this life. I have hundreds of times seen dying patients speak to people who died earlier. Dying people all say they are met by deceased loved ones."[15]

It might be just considered an interesting sideline of Kubler-Ross' work for her to speak to such groups if her tone were not so mystical and utterly absorbed into the phenomena she reports. Further, we have difficulty believing in the objectivity of a scientist who casually reports interviews with a "spirit guide," and company. If the partisan journal accurately reported the reaction of the crowd, we are stunned by the emotional excess of the medical professionals also.

Finally, Kubler-Ross forthrightly reported an interview with one of her dead patients! The startling encounter was detailed in the San Francisco Sunday Examiner and Chronicle, Nov. 14, 1976 (Section B, p. 6-7). We are more interested in the supposed purpose of this unique visitation than its mystic character. It seems that Kubler-Ross was considering giving up her research among the dying people some ten years ago, but the dead patient "materialized" and spurred her on:

She (the "deceased") said she knew I was considering giving up my work with dying patients and that she came to tell me not to give it up...

69

(This incident) came at a crossroads where I would have made the wrong decision if I hadn't listened to her.

Certainly any living person would be thunderstruck by such a manifestation (except a medium, who would accept it as "all in a day's work"), but Kubler-Ross' reaction was in a religious context. She continued her work among the dying patients, according to the advice of the apparition, eventually exulting that:

> The work with dying patients has also helped me to find my own religious identity, to know that there is life after death and to know that we will be reborn (i.e., reincarnated) again one day in order to complete the tasks we have not been able to or willing to complete in this life-time.[16]

There's that occult echo again, similar to the very words of the resuscitated Arthur Ford.

In most unscientific fashion, Kubler-Ross seemingly urges us all toward the occult. In her forward to Raymond Moody's book, she says that we have reached an "era of transition in our society." We must "have the courage to open new doors" and admit our scientific tools are inadequate "for many of these new investigations."

Dr. Moody cannot be convicted of so bold an interest in the spirit world, but he does have an involvement. Alexander and Albrecht state:

> While Raymond Moody displays his metaphysical loyalties more clearly in print than Kubler-Ross does, less is known about his actual background and spiritual history. Tal Brooke was coincidentally a friend and fellow student of Moody at the University of Virginia. At the time Brooke was an avid and omnivorous student of esoteric philosophies, whether Eastern-religious, occult or psychic. This was a fascina-

tion which Moody shared, and this common interest was, in fact, the major basis for their companionship. Brooke (who became a Christian in India in 1971) relates that Moody claimed that he regularly conversed with a spirit being (which he identified as "God") who manifested primarily as a voice in his head.[17]

Also, the sources Dr. Moody selects as corroborating evidence of his findings involve the occult as well. "The Tibetan Book of the Dead," a classic and potent occult volume, and the experiences of medium Emanuel Swedenborg are both cited as source materials for information about life after death. Moody utilizes the works of Plato, who also was involved in the occult,[18] and even the Bible, covering all possible bases, in his search for similarities to clinical death cases. (There are certainly none in the Bible as we will explain below.)

The Tibetan view of life and death teaches typical Eastern mysticism — that life and death are one entity — and seeks to instruct the dying toward a safe passage.[19] Swedenborg taught a heartening, but unbiblical, doctrine of universalism — that all men would ultimately be saved and that basic Biblical doctrines were "satanical tenets."[20] He felt, "Any predestination except to heaven is contrary to the Divine love," in opposition to Bible admonition.[21] His description of the after-death state based on his own mediumistic experiences, was exactly the same as those Moody details today.[22]

Again, while appreciating the difficulty of utilizing truly scientific methods on so unique an area as life after death, we do not think that material from such sources constitutes a scientific inquiry. We don't mean to condemn either Kubler-Ross or Moody for bad study habits or some sort of religious heresy; that is not our objective. But we do feel on safe ground to say that what they have advanced is not scientific, and not done, ultimately, in the interests of science at all.

Neither do we mean to single out these two particular researchers, since virtually everyone at work in this strange inquiry trips over the occult at some point in his journey. We have indicated the obviously unscientific conclusions of other researchers in earlier chapters and the unreliability in general of research with the resuscitated "dead."

We mean only to make one thing clear: We have seen no real proof at all of people returning from the dead, and as to the experiences that they believe they had, there is a biblical explanation as old as the appearance of the serpent.

LIGHT ON LIGHT

Now let's shed some more light on that Being of Light.

We shouldn't leave this discussion of the occult connection without looking more carefully at this nearly universal experience of those who say they have come back from the beyond. The Being of Light interests us very much.

We're not totally convinced that the Being of Light is one of the good guys. Even though he is often interpreted as Jesus Himself, or some good angel, we're not entirely sold on him.

We think he's sort of a demon in disguise, if you will.

Moody actually gives the demon theory some mention in his book, but he rejects it on the grounds of the almost universal misconception that demons must appear as evil beings and talk about evil all the time.[23] Since the Being of Light is always so accommodating a tour guide he doesn't usually get credit for being a negative spirit.

We have noted, however, that the devil's chief ploy is just that — to appear as a good guy. And we are backed up in the scriptures, the only reliable source of information about the devil. II Cor. 11:13-14 (Amplified) states that ". . .even Satan masquerades as an angel of light. . .and his servants as ministers of righteousness." Deception has always been the devil's right hand, if we are to believe the scriptures.

72

Moody does say, to his credit, "It seems to me that the best way of distinguishing between God-directed and Satan-directed experiences would be to see what the person involved does and says after his experience,"[24] and we subscribe to that. Jesus said much the same, more succinctly ("You shall know them by their fruits." Matthew 7:16 KJV). But Moody's estimation of the character of his subjects after the life-and-death experience seems too optimistic. He calls them "loving and forgiving," which is all to the good. But we have seen that some tend to have that missionary feeling toward life after death. Matson reports "they feel definitely they have been given a mission to prepare others who have not had their opportunity for the next great step in life — which is death."[25] With all good intentions, they go about spreading false doctrine, as it were, about dying. They teach that Swedenborgian universalism — we're all going to heaven — or that Kubler-Ross "glow of awe and wonder." They relax people into a false reassurance about meeting God, and they tend to direct the average person's attention away from God and His expressed view of life after death in the Bible.

Being loving and forgiving by itself falls short of God's minimum for true life after death, as we will show below.

In the content of the Being of Light's attitude and message[26] to his new acquaintances is a devilish, if positive-sounding, doctrine:

1. Don't worry about death. Everything will be okay.
2. Death is an advance to the next level of existence.
3. There is no judgment, despite the review of the subject's life. The Being of Light is most accepting.
4. The Being of Light is pleasant to be with.
5. Love others more. Gain new knowledge.
6. Good works are important. There is no Biblical repentance necessary.
7. Heaven and Hell are not mentioned.
8. Christ and salvation are not mentioned.[27]

Satan would have had a much easier time with Job — and he would with all of us — if that doctrine were widely believed. And actually, it *is* pretty widely believed, unbiblical as it is; and Satan *is* having a pretty easy time of things these days, it would appear.

But obviously the Being of Light who teaches the above list is no angel, we might say, or at least not a holy angel. And to interpret him as being Christ is unconscionable. Jesus and the unfallen angels, the Scriptures tell us plainly, are concerned about sin and warn unbelievers about the coming judgment. They teach the gospel which sees death as the wages of sin, not a step upward.[28] They do praise love and knowledge, but certainly not as the spiritual purpose of earthly life. True repentance — virtually the theme of the entire Bible — is central to life and death. It is not being sorry for one's sins, but a turning to Christ and away from sin.

The Being of Light may well represent one of those seemingly good spirits who can turn on his contactees. People who have dabbled in the occult and achieved the level of being guided by "familiar (friendly) spirits" found their spirit guides very hard to disobey or discard later on. Those who have come to a sincere belief in Christ are rescued, as it were, from spirits who have undertaken to completely dominate the personality, but the matter is problematical at best. The spirits can be treacherous. Former medium Raphael Gasson states:

> I realize just how much of a (friend) he was when this familiar spirit attempted to kill me when it became obvious I was out to denounce Spiritualism.[29]

He also gives his personal conclusions after decades of personal involvement:

> Spiritualism is an attempt to communicate with what are presumed to be the spirits of the dead. Those who indulge in this cult give themselves

up to demons, who pose as "spirit guides" and "loved ones," and Spiritualists become ready to give obedience to what are actually demons whether they realize it or not....

The communicating spirit invariably gives all the required proof quite easily by mentioning intimate things that the inquirer may not know himself, but which later prove to be true. Sometimes the communicating spirit will pretend to be an evil spirit by making deliberate mistakes and this gives a good excuse for adherents of this cult when anything goes wrong to put it down to the agency of evil spirits, confusing the contacts....

It is this uncanny knowledge of past and present events and activities that convinces so many people that they are literally communicating with departed relatives and friends and guides. Naturally this knowledge is one of the most effective weapons in the armory of the hosts of darkness and will be wielded by them to its fullest extent, and the demons themselves will see to it that their knowledge of us is perfected in every way possible, and used with the utmost skill and exactitude to accomplish their purpose. [30]

We could cite many more cases — personal testimonies — of those who have wrestled with friendly spirits, not unlike the Being of Light. They are horrifying.

The Being of Light has his work cut out for him. Not everybody is so ready to buy his magic.

TAKE YOUR CHOICE

In the next two chapters we will discuss something like two different life-styles. One has to do with the thinking that death is no problem, and we're all headed for a happy ending. The other is strictly the Biblical view of death.

With the former, we'd like to sound the alarm. If you've read this far, you are probably not interested in encountering anything occult anyway, but we feel that there are certain new and unfamiliar dangers to this whole life-after-death deception. Believing even vaguely in the reported clinical experiences, we feel, can have serious consequences even for Bible-believing people. More than one sincere Christian has totally bought the fact that the Being of Light is none other than Jesus Christ and, unfortunately, those people are in a perfect position to be fooled.

As to the Biblical view of death, it surprises most people. The Bible considers death to be the result of something that went wrong in the human condition. It is abnormal, and it doesn't really have to occur at all!

More on that later. Let us first see if a bad tree can bear any good fruit.

1. *Psychic* Magazine, article by John White, ''What the Dying See,'' Sept.-Oct. 1976, p. 40. Used by permission.

2. C. S. Lewis, *Screwtape Letters*, (New York: Macmillan Co.) 1971, p. 23.

3. Arthur Ford, *The Life Beyond Death*, (New York: G. P. Putnam's Sons) ©1971, p. 144-6.

4. Ibid., p. 158.

5. For Biblical evidences see H. Morris, *Many Infallible Proofs* (San Diego: Creation Life) 1976; C. Pinnock, *Set Forth Your Case* (Chicago: Moody) 1971; F. Schaeffer, *He Is There and He Is Not Silent* (Wheaton, Ill.: Tyndale House) 1972; R. D. Wilson, *A Scientific Investigation of the Old Testament*; (Chicago: Moody Press) 1967; Norman Geisler, *Christian Apologetics*, (1977); R. L. Wysong, *The Creation Evolution Controversy* (East Lansing, Mich.: Inquiry Press) 1976, Box 1884, zip 48823.

6. Archie Matson, *Afterlife*, p. 74.

7. Ibid., p. 76.

8. Ena Twigg, *The Woman Who Stunned The World: Ena Twigg*, (New York: Manor) 1973, Ch. 11; Jane Roberts, *Seth Speaks*, (New Jersey: Prentice Hall) 1972, Chs. 9-10; *National Enquirer*, Feb. 1, 1977; Ruth Montgomery, *A World Beyond*, (Fawcett Crest) 1972, Chs. 6-10.

9. That this is true can be seen by an examination of their published writings. The following are representative — most all have been or are involved in mediumship or other forms of the

occult. If there was no previous occult involvement, there usually is after. Note the following impact on authors who have researched and published books on this topic: Dr. Kubler-Ross — a medium with spirit guides, who does astral travel, believes in reincarnation from her past lives experience; Dr. Raymond Moody will now "look more closely" at occult writings (*Life After Life*, p. 9); Dr. Karlis Osis — a parapsychologist to begin with, finds great confirmation of the occult, mediumistic world view after his research; Archie Matson — a liberal minister, now an advocate of mediumism and occult practices (*Afterlife*, p. 35, 57-73, 92); Harold Sherman — occultist, advocates necromancy via meditation (*You Live After Death*, Fawcett, 1972, p. 156); David Wheeler (*Journey to the Other Side*, New York: Grosset & Dunlop) 1976, Ch. 15; Jean-Baptiste Delacour, (*Glimpses of the Beyond*, New York: Delacorte) 1974, Ch. 15-17; S. Ralph Harlow, (*A Life After Death*, New York: Manor) 1973; Suzy Smith, (*Life Is Forever*, New York: Dell) 1977; Allen Spraggett (*The Case for Immortality*, New York: Signet) 1975, Chs. 2, 4, 5, 7; Hans Holzer, (*Life After Death*, New York: Bobbs-Merrill) 1969, Chs. 3. 6-8, 10; A. J. Smith (*Immortality, The Scientific Evidence*, New York: Prentice Hall) 1954, Chs. 8, 12, 13 were all either involved in the occult or moved toward it as a result of their research. One of the key early researchers in this area, Frederick Myers, stated in his famous *Human Personality and its Survival of Bodily Death*, (New York: Longmans, Green & Co.) 1935, p. 7, how indebted he was to the spiritualists: "How much I owe to certain observations made by members of this group — how often my own conclusions concur with conclusions at which they have previously arrived."

10. John W. Montgomery, *Principalities and Powers*, (Minneapolis: Bethany) 1973, p. 149.

11. Kurt Koch, *The Devil's Alphabet*, (Grand Rapids: Kregel) 1969, p. 7.

12. *Yoga Journal*, Sept.-Oct. 1976, p. 18-20.

13. E.g., *Yoga Journal*, Jan.-Feb. 1977, p. 40-1.

14. *Yoga Journal*, Sept.-Oct. 1976, "Elizabeth Kubler-Ross: Messenger of Love" p. 18-20.

15. *National Enquirer*, Feb. 1, 1977.

16. Elizabeth Kubler-Ross, *Death: The Final Stage of Growth* (New Jersey: Prentice Hall) 1975, p. 119.

17. "Thanatology, Death and Dying" *Spiritual Counterfeits Project*, P. O. Box 4308, Berkeley, Ca. 94704.

18. Jeffrey Mishlove, *The Roots of Consciousness* (New York: Random House) 1975, p. 13, 14, 25-6.

19. W. Y. Evans-Wentz, *The Tibetan Book of the Dead*, (New York: Oxford University Press) 1976, preface numbers 1 and 2 by Evans-Wentz.

20. Emanuel Swedenborg, *The True Christian Religion*, (New York: E. P. Dutton) 1936, p. 667-669.

21. Emanuel Swedenborg, *The Divine Providence*, (New York: the Swedenborg Foundation) 1931, p. 505.

22. Emanuel Swedenborg, *Heaven and Its Wonders and Hell*, (New York: Swedenborg Foundation) 1940, p. 447-8.
23. Moody, *Life After Life*, p. 107-8.
24. Ibid., p. 107.
25. Matson, *Afterlife*, p. 41.
26. This includes other spirits, as well.
27. Moody, *Life After Life*, pp. 45-53, 70.
28. See Luke 2:18-25; 15:20; Acts 5:20; I Peter 1:12; Rev. 14:6-12; 19:10; 22:9, etc.
29. Raphael Gasson, *The Challenging Counterfeit*, (Plainfield, N.J.: Logos) © 1970, p. 83.
30. Ibid., pp. 32, 99, 101.

"The most powerful sorcerer I have ever met is the shaman Alualuk whom, as I have already mentioned, I met in Alaska when visiting the Eskimo tribe to which he belongs. This shaman even possessed the occult power to raise heathen people from the dead. One such person who he raised to life again lived a further ten years. However, Alualuk was soundly converted to Christ and as a result of his conversion he lost his magical powers. When I asked him, 'Whose power did you use to do all these things?' he replied, 'The power of the devil of course.' He admitted, though, that he had never possessed any power over real and genuine Christians.

"Throughout the testimonies of former magicians the same comforting message continually recurs. Jesus Christ has defeated all the powers of darkness. The true believer is therefore forever guarded by Him from all the devices of the devil. However, a merely nominal Christian who carelessly comes into contact with the occult is in serious danger of falling prey to a satanic ban."

Kurt Koch, *Occult Bondage and Deliverance*,
p. 22

"The spirits I encountered at seances were, for the most part, very moralistic."

Former medium, Victor Ernest,
I Talked with Spirits, p. 36, 38

6

The Satan Factor

If we think we're going to confront God when we die we tend to live accordingly. If we think we're going to confront an all-accepting Being of Light, we will also live accordingly.

Truly our concept of death deeply affects our way of life.

An occult view of death — whether through psychic "travel" to an existing world beyond the grave, or a reincarnation philosophy — tends to move an individual toward an occult view of life. The belief in the presence of a spirit world after death tends to bring that spirit world right into this life. The world of the occult tends to visit people who believe in it.

There is an optimistic tendency these days for people to think that everything supernatural comes from God. If something happens that cannot be explained scientifically, then God must have caused it to happen. And in these incredible days of UFO's, endless cults, spiritists and mediums, prophets of many stripes and world-saving "messiahs" coming out of newly invented churches by the dozens, God is getting far more blame than He ever deserved.

God sent Rev. Moon, say some. God sent us Maharishi and his anesthetizing meditation. God sent the "Divine Light," through the youthful "Perfect Messiah," Majaraj Ji. Hare Krishna proclaims God, Baha'i proclaims God and LSD trippers see God all the time. God gives new prophecies to an endless stream of antibiblical seers, and God helps mediums arrange interviews with the dead.

Finally, God is setting up a general evacuation from a dying earth via UFO's. We shall all go to another, happier place out there among the stars, if we pay our advance fee to the local cult and make our reservations.

It's enough to make God bring down the curtain on this present age altogether, and that's what He said He'll do, biblically speaking.

Actually these rather modernistic ideas hark back to heresies as ancient as the court of Pharoah. Pharoah's magicians were able to duplicate in some measure the miracles Moses demonstrated from God (Ex. 7) but Moses, unfortunately for the Egyptian population, outdistanced them finally. Men have ever complained of an all-powerful but mischievous God who made them sin, made them sick, made them unhappy and ultimately made them die. God has invariably gotten the credit for man's failings, and He is more lately getting the credit for some of man's most ungodly and most ingenious solutions to the human condition.

Now that man is intruding into the big question of life and death itself — definitely God's province — God is being remanufactured as a character of infinite benevolence who passes out forgiveness wholesale through a host of friendly assistants.

God still has a very good name and identifying one's ideas with God gives them a certain charisma. But that certainly doesn't make God responsible for every demonstration of supernatural power on earth. We think most of these supernatural manifestations being seen today come from the other side instead. We think they're demonic demonstrations, and they're to be expected as God's plan for this age comes to a close.

DEMON POWER

Most people figure that if demons really do exist they do nothing but evil. The trouble with *The Exorcist* and *The Omen* was not that they failed to indict the demons for being awful to human beings, but that they failed to point out that demons are often very nice to human beings. Demons should get more credit; they're often the "nicest" spiritual beings around.

People also fail to appreciate that demons create some very fine things. They don't, according to the scriptures, invariably wreak evil upon unsuspecting men. In fact, they assist willing men in doing some mighty works — some really exciting and creative accomplishments. Pharoah was impressed with the powers of his court magicians, and he was able to make a good case against Moses and God through their production of snakes from dead matter, et al. Pharoah became so impressed that it ultimately cost Egypt the death of every firstborn son to discover what was of God and what was of the devil.

We might digress for just a moment to note some accomplishments produced by occultists, obviously through their guiding spirits. We cannot fail, like Pharoah, to be impressed.

We classify the following accomplishments as demonic because they involve unbiblical communications and are achieved by cultic subjects utilizing supernatural means (e.g., "automatic writing," Ouija Boards, trances and the like). Also, the accomplishments are normally achieved by those not competent in preparation or talent or experience for such high-level productions. We document each accomplishment below in its original source of verification.

First there was the magnificent prose of Mrs. John Curran, said to rival Shakespeare. With a Ouija Board and automatic writing (where the pen is guided by a force outside the subject's will) housewife Curran produced some 3 million words![1] We stress that the writing was of fine quality, fascinating to read.

Seventy-five thousand separate communications from "the dead" have been recorded on magnetic tape by one source to date. Up to six different languages are utilized in one sentence![2]

High quality philosophical and religious writings have been produced by "dictation" from the spirit world. The 10,000-page Seth Phenomena is representative. Some analysts include the Koran and the Book of Mormon in this category. Exceptionally advanced and useful mathematical formulae have also "arrived" by dictation to those normally not qualified in that area.[3]

Some 400 fine musical compositions were dictated to Rosemary Brown, hardly a composer, by Liszt, Chopin, Mozart, Bach, etc. The styles are recognizably those of the composers. (Some rock musicians claim to be mediums and to receive musical compositions from the spirit world designed to foster communication between the listeners and the spirits.)[4]

Paintings have been created through "automatic painting," guided by spirits, according to the earthly artists. So have some quality dramas. Several volumes of a lost Egyptian language came to one recipient and the language eventually proved genuine.[5]

Literature has been dictated in the style of noted authors — Jack London, Charles Dickens, etc.[6]

A host of advanced technical "gifts" of the spirits include "psychic surgery" (operations done in a trance state with crude instruments), UFO's, complex machines and all sorts of highly modernistic devices to save time and labor. The Xerox copier is said to have originated from occult sources[7] (with the required favor of donating a great deal of the financial proceeds to parapsychological research).

Fully solid human beings — not apparitions — have appeared on occasion. They are duplicates of dead people, usually, down to the color of the eyes and the bluish veins in the skin (though the beings are reportedly cold to the touch).[8]

Now admittedly some of the above seems hard to believe even if people have testified to it all in writing. And anyway, why would the demons be so helpful, so creative and so downright obvious about it all? Aren't demons just supposed to go around scaring people to death?

Well, of course, that's our point. Demons can be counted on to work at good "public relations," if we may. Modern human beings are far too skeptical to fall for dreams and miracles; they must be impressed by more than Pharoah's snakes. And so we're getting quality. The devil cares enough to send the very best.

TEST THE SPIRITS

Because God well knows that the devil is capable of some very good works the Bible admonishes us to "test the spirits." There's good and bad in the spirit world, and the differences between spirits are not easy to discern.

We wish to follow Jesus' logic: A bad tree cannot bear good fruit, according to the Lord. And because of the impressive positive nature of some of the demonic manifestations being experienced today we want to be especially cautious in our testing.

We want to really squeeze that fruit. And we want to give special examination to that latest and most ambitious phenomenon of demonic demonstrations — life-after-death.

We have already noted that the folks who return from the dead, or wherever, have a very positive attitude about their experience. They no longer fear death, and they may want to get others into that position. What could be a happier thought than a peaceful journey awaiting us all in the beyond?

But there's where we get suspicious. The Bible clearly indicates that a happy journey in the beyond is possible for everyone, but only upon a certain condition. Salvation, by God's method, is necessary for all men if we are to have a positive experience after this life.

When we find a worldly doctrine disagreeing with a Biblical doctrine, we get very uneasy. We want to test the spirits that originated the unbiblical doctrine.

The most bothersome part of these otherwise pleasant life-after-death experiences is that people who held a traditional view of heaven and hell previously, tend to discard it after their interview in the next world. Moody states:

> In most cases the reward-punishment model of the afterlife is abandoned and disavowed, even by many who had been accustomed to thinking in those terms.

It is replaced with a new understanding of the world and the next life — "not unilateral judgment, but rather cooperative development toward the ultimate end of self-realization."[9] The very concept of salvation — of man approaching a righteous God through a substitutionary atonement — is done away with. The Biblical plan for life after death (or, as the bible expresses it, eternal life) tends to become subverted and abandoned by those who sample this other, more easy concept.

The mission of Jesus Christ is utterly forgotten by those who get caught up in this latest demonic deception.

Now we are not the only researchers to come to the conclusion of demonic activity being active in the clinical-death phenomena. Brooks Alexander and Mark Albrecht state:

> Since the spiritual stakes are so high in this entire issue of life after death, we must also be prepared to consider one of the clearest Scriptural possibilities, even though it is one of the most difficult Biblical themes to handle responsibly. In view of the necromantic connections of the leading thanatologists, the obvious

Biblical inference must be drawn — that there is the potential of outright demonic collusion and otherworldly manipulation of mental states.

Scientifically speaking, there is nothing to negate such a possibility. In fact, so little is known of the interrelationship between the neurological, the psychic and the spiritual that "science" would be hard put to say anything at all that was not essentially speculation. It is common knowledge that the experience of a thought or emotion is the subjective correlate of a series of electro-chemical events which take place within the brain...

Under the circumstances, then, it is at least reasonable to suggest that if neurological events can impinge upon the psychic and spiritual realms, the influence might run in the other direction as well, so that spiritual beings could influence the conditions of human consciousness. (The famous neurosurgeon, Dr. Wilder Penfield demonstrated that by proper stimulation of certain brain areas, patients could relive forgotten events with precise, complete detail — similar to Moody's "review.")

Biblically speaking, we know by revelation that the nature of our spiritual warfare as Christians is determined by a clash of *personal* wills — God's will vs. that of His adversary. The implications of this are that "evil" should be seen not as some impersonal negativity...but as embodied in a corrupt personal entity possessing intelligence and will. This entity exists in dimensions beyond the space-time realm we live in, but is capable of interacting with it. Since it possesses *purposes*, this entity is quite capable of acting *strategically* in behalf of hidden objectives, i.e., deceitfully...

Paul warns us that Satan's emissaries regularly disguise themselves, and that Satan himself appears as an "angel of light" (II Cor. 11:14 KJV). This is a characteristic we can readily discern in the standard spiritist refrains on love, joy and peace within—notes which are eerily echoed by Kubler-Ross and Moody. The appeal of thanatology is not surprising when we realize that death is everyone's ultimate concern...This fact, integrated with a subtle yet direct dismantling of the gospel, makes the entire subject a prime candidate for satanic meddling. [10]

OUT OF THE BODY

Basic to occult experiences is out-of-the-body travel. This is an old, old story: that the human spirit may leave the body and go elsewhere, returning later on, was the theme of many a drama, myth and religious legend throughout man's history.

Thousands of mediums utilize "astral projection" — traveling out of the body, or more simply referred to as OBE (out-of-the-body experience). Their spirits travel to the spirit world in this manner. (It should be said that it becomes extremely difficult to interpret whether a medium's spirit really goes anywhere at all. Many a skilled hypnotist can cause ordinary folk to "travel" somewhere by inducing their mental processes through suggestion. But we'll utilize the OBE idea for the sake of discussion).

Folks accomplish some very long trips via OBE. UFO contactees, those lucky enough to be in touch with "whoever-it-is" driving those "whatever-they-ares" over our heads, have gone to the Moon, Mars, Venus and elsewhere through the largesse of the UFO masters (see *UFO's: What on Earth Is Happening?* by the authors, Harvest House, 1975). Occultists like Paul Twitchell of the Eckankar cult and Geoffrey King of the "Mighty-I-Am" cult report some really hair-raising trips, exploring everything from underground civilizations to dozens of spiritual-world existences run by various deities. The Hare Krishna folks report astral travel to planets with vast oceans of milk, or for the party people, liquor.[11]

OBEs are endlessly intriguing, but they present the classic case of "a nice place to visit but I wouldn't want to live there." The problem is, people dabbling in the occult to the point of OBE have their troubles closing the door again. People just don't forget about an experience like a trip through the spiritual realm, any more than they can forget about having seen life after death.

And that's what we want to say about OBEs. They seem to be the same thing.

OBE reports are indistinguishable from life-after-death reports. The two are just an occult matter of out-of-the-body travel to somewhere very fascinating. A trip into the next life may be even more galvanizing than a mere trip to another planet, but they amount to the same trip.

We just seriously wonder in many cases whether anybody really ever went anywhere.

Now there is a negative side to this whole matter of OBEs which is very obvious. People merely dabbling in the occult out of curiosity may take some trips they never wanted to take. In the manner that transcendental meditation affects some people very adversely, getting a grip on their consciousness so that they have trouble "returning," an OBE can affect people very deeply, making life complex and scary. In the authors' *The Transcendental Explosion* (Harvest House, 1976), documentation is given of extremely adverse reactions to TM leading, in some cases, to utter psychosis. In the same manner, we believe, out-of-the-body experiences hold extreme dangers.

Another obvious negative about the OBEs is that they make life into a picture of spiritual realms, where death is just one more place to be. The very human fear of death, as we have said, becomes relaxed, and any spiritual conceptions about life becomes extremely distorted.

We think the new life-after-death experience amounts to just another, more fancy, OBE. We think Satan's purpose here is to take a fact of life with little tie-in to the occult world — normal death by disease or injury — and imbue it with a new spiritual flavor. Thus imbued, death even becomes attractive.

Death, with that fascinating journey that it becomes under the influence of Satan, is no longer to be taken negatively. That's a remarkable accomplishment, even on the part of our formidable enemy.

DEATH: THE GOOD LIFE

Death becomes a better life than life this way.

Truly we become worth more dead than alive.

It is purely human to want to explore some new world even if that world is only obtainable via OBE, or other occultic means. It is likely that nobody who ever got satisfaction at a seance went to only one. Having contacted the dead, one would want to continue such contact, assuming the experience was positive, which it usually is. We have only to consult those who report the after-death experience to understand that they actually look forward to dying again, and the next time remaining over there.

Now, if a person has one out-of-the-body experience (and OBEs are not so scary or unimaginable — our dreams often cast us as looking at ourselves from outside our own bodies) he wants to have another. And in this way he gets steadily sucked into the occult. In older days hearing a ghost say, *"Whoo, Whoo!"* was sufficient to intrigue people, but in these times we actually get to travel — even to die and return.

But it's still the same old seance, with perhaps graver consequences. When people lose their God concept we must be concerned. When the Bible is made to look inaccurate or mythical, we know where to look for the villain of the piece.

And in virtually all cases that's just what happens.

Seasoned OBE traveler Robert Monroe, who has taken literally thousands of trips to who-knows-where, testifies to this utter loss of a God concept. He reports:

To date, in twelve years of non-physical activities (i.e., spiritual travel) I find no evidence to substantiate the biblical notions of God and afterlife in a place called heaven.[12]

And, in a considerable display of his sense of loss:

I sat down and cried, great deep sobs as I have never cried before, because then I knew without any qualification or future hope of change that the God of my childhood, of the churches ...was not as we worshipped Him to be...that for the rest of my life, I would "suffer" the loss of this illusion.[13]

Despite Monroe's attitude in terming scripture "biblical notions" and God "this illusion," he betrays a tremendous feeling of loss and we don't wonder. God is probably not worshipped perfectly accurately in many churches and much of the biblical material on life after death may be widely misunderstood, but death as described via the OBE is literally a Hell of a substitute!

Mediums who get converted to Christ become convinced their spirit guides were really demons. Monroe relates a fascinating occurrence on one of his OBEs that leads credence to this idea of demons imitating the dead. At the time, he was being "attacked" by weird little humanoids who kept crawling on his back:

Then, as I was trying to hold off the first, a second climbed on my back! Holding the first off with one hand, I reached back and yanked the second off me, and floated over into the center of the office, holding one in each hand, screaming for help. I got a good look at each, and as I looked, each turned into a good facsimile of one of my two daughters...I seemed to know immediately that this was a deliberate camouflage on their parts to create emotional confusion in me and call upon my love for my daughters to prevent my doing anything more to them.

The moment I realized the trick, the two no longer appeared to be my daughters....However, I got the impression that they were both amused, as if there was nothing I could do to harm them. By this time, I was sobbing for help.[14]

Monroe has gone on to form a M-5000 "clinic" for dying people with Dr. Kubler-Ross in Kansas City.[15] The legitimacy of the OBE established in his mind, he is attempting to prepare people for death by training them to achieve astral projection, or out-of-the-body travel. Incredible as all this sounds, Monroe explains matter-of-factly:

Given three months, we can easily train a person to achieve out-of-the-body experience and change his concept of death and establish a beachhead where he's going.[16]

The clinic is a great success, with more applicants than can be handled, at this writing. Over 600 people have graduated from the course (where are they now?) and the program is ready to go national.

Alexander and Albrecht give us more information:

This is the outward, technological face of M-5000. But there is a deeper reality behind the scenes, as was revealed in a recent interview with Tal Brooke, who participated in Monroe's investigations while an undergraduate at the University of Virginia in the 1960s:

Q: How were you involved with Monroe's OBE experiments?

A: I worked with Robert Monroe between 1966 and 1969. There was a period of about a year in which I was going out there at least three times a week. At that time he was evolving his tape technique, and he was learning it from "the other side." In other words, he would get into an OBE state at night, and he would talk with various "beings of light" which tutored him on the technology of eliciting OBEs in other people.

Q: So he has been involved with direct spiritist contact with supernatural beings...

A: Yes; where Monroe fits into the picture is that his breakthrough may be in the area of using technology to produce mediumship....[17]

Death researcher Dr. Charles Garfield validates this latter idea saying the initial research (e.g., by Moody etc.) is not proof and that we will have to "develop more sophisticated ways of detecting whether there is really communication with the dead."[18]

This particular clinic is not the only place where a philosophy of preparing for death by spiritual travel is practiced. Mediums have been doing it for years, of course. Author Herbert Greenhouse thinks of the OBE as useful in the preparation for death connection; in his *The Astral Journey* he states, "Its main purpose may be to practice the act of dying and in so doing, remove the fear of death."[19]

THE BIBLE TELLS US SO

For those of us who want to go on practicing the act of living, we're now going to turn to the Bible. The scriptures, we shall find, predicted all of this — or at least warned of increased demon activity, false doctrines, phony saviors and the like at the end of this age.

93

We find, as Bible believers, that all of these new odds and ends about life after death fit a pattern. Demon activity is ingenious and various, and very effective on the uninformed. But it has certain outstanding characteristics which can be pegged easily with a little application of the scriptures.

We reject the scientific notions about these new experiences because we have seen that those working at the research are not really treating the matter scientifically at all. We reject the whole idea of trusting in human experience, especially secondhand experiences of a sensational kind, instead of God's Word. We reject the increasing social movement toward the occult and away from both the Bible and common sense.

The Word of God has quite a bit to say about death — not only how to prepare for it, but how to avoid it altogether!

Read on.

1. W. F. Prince, *The Case of Patience Worth*, (University Books, 1964).
2. K. Raudive, *Breakthrough: An Amazing Experiment in Electronic Communication With the Dead* (1971).
3. L. Pauwels and J. Bergier, *The Morning of the Magicians*, (Avon, 1969) p. 360-62. Jane Roberts. *Seth Speaks*, (Prentice Hall, 1972).
4. Rosemary Brown, *Unfinished Symphonies*, (New York: William Morrow and Co., 1971). *Psychic* Magazine, February, 1976, pages 25-8; *New Age Journal*, November, 1976, p. 17; Psychic music records, Burchett Bros. 1976.
5. F. H. Wood, *This Egyptian Miracle* (David McKay, 1939). *The Yoga Journal*, Jan.-Feb., 1977, page 3, see note 6, Woodcock.
6. Some may have been mediums themselves — cf. Anspacher, *The Challenge of the Unknown*, 1947, p. 107-126; Hestor Nowden, *Psychic Messages from Oscar Wilde;* D. O. Roberts, C. Woodcock, *The Elizabethean Episode, N. B.;* A. C. Doyle, *The Edge of the Unknown*, (Berkley: Medallion) 1968, p. 85-100; etc.
7. Gina Cerminara, *Insights for the Age of Aquarius* (Wheaton, Ill: Theosophical) 1976, p. 203.
8. Gasson, p. 134, 141.
9. Moody, *Life After Life*, p. 70.
10. *Spiritual Counterfeits Project Journal*, April 1977, from SCP, P.O. Box 4308, Berkley, Calif. 94704.

12. Robert Monroe, *Journeys Out of the Body*, (Garden City, New York: Anchor/Doubleday) 1971, p. 116.
13. Ibid., p. 262.
14. Ibid., p. 138-9.
15. *National Observer*, May 15. 1977, p. 10; *New York*, Jan. 3, 1977, p. 66 +.
16. Ibid.
17. *Spiritual Counterfeits Project Journal*, April 1977, cf. note 10.
18. *National Observer*, May 15, 1976, p. 10.
19. Herbert Greenhouse, *The Astral Journey*, (New York: Avon) 1976, p. 322.

"'I'm ready to accept Jesus as a great moral teacher, but I don't accept His claim to be God.' That is the one thing we must not say. A man who was merely a man and said the sort of things Jesus said would not be a great moral teacher. He would either be a lunatic — on a level with the man who says he is a poached egg — or else he would be the Devil of Hell. You must make your choice. Either this man was, and is, the Son of God; or else a madman or something worse. You can shut Him up for a fool, you can spit at Him and kill Him as a demon; or you can fall at His feet and call Him Lord and God. But let us not come with any patronizing nonsense about His being a great human teacher. He has not left that open to us. He did not intend to."

C. S. Lewis, *Mere Christianity*,
Book 2, Chapter 3, Macmillan, © 1943,
1945, 1952, 1971

"The historical difficulty of giving for the life, sayings and influence of Jesus any explanation that is not harder than the Christian explanation, is very great. The discrepancy between the depth and sanity and (let me add) *shrewdness* of His moral teaching and the rampant megalomania which must be behind His theological teaching unless He is indeed God, has never been satisfactorily gotten over. Hence, the non-Christian hypotheses succeed one another with the restless fertility of bewilderment."

C. S. Lewis, *Miracles*, Fontana 1960, p. 113

7

He Is Risen!

There are ultimately only two reactions to death and they depend on one's concept of God.

Those who believe in God and His biblical plan for the salavation of men do not really fear death. According to the scriptures they have nothing to fear.

The other reaction comes from those who do not believe in God, or at least do not count on biblical salvation. Their view of life is materialistic, and they invariably fear death. Death is their dread enemy. Even those who have led discouraged lives, or suffered painful, debilitating diseases at the end, deeply resent death.

This secular response to death is universal, cutting across all cultures and all philosophies. Man has desperately searched outside of God, for a way to explain death or to ease the fear. But to be faithless is to hate death. In the final analysis death is our worst enemy, our most fearful torment in this life, our most excruciating experience, if we face it without God.

We must all die. But we need not all fear that fact.

It's getting somewhat more fashionable these days to quote the Bible, or at least to refer to its ideas in discussing modern life. The world's least-read best-seller is seemingly coming into vogue as a useful book of philosophy, if not surprisingly dependable prophecy.

And the Bible comments expertly on death.

Who but God would know the real story on death? If we can give God just an iota of credit for creation, He must know a thing or two about its other end, extinction. And as a matter of fact, the Bible treats death at great length; one might almost say that death is the central topic of the scriptures — or at least the avoidance of death's consequences. "Life—How to Get It; How to Use It" might well be an alternate title for the New Testament (Jn. 10:10) and life cannot really be discussed apart from death.

The Bible certainly agrees with the prevailing thoughts about death. The Bible says death is an enemy, an abnormal condition. Death makes slaves out of free men. Hebrews 2:15 certifies that those who are saved "through fear of death were subject to slavery all their lives." And we all must die, the Bible attests. We all sin, and "The wages of sin is death." (Rom. 6:23 KJV)

But the Bible gives a solution, of course. This is the ultimate purpose of the Bible. The Bible talks about death so that it can instruct us about life. Pagan and materialistic philosophies leave us wanting where death is concerned. Communists answer death by saying it's unimportant; soon world communism will be victorious and life will be sublime. Materialists boast of scientific achievement — replacement of organs and other medical means to prolong life — but death still prevails. The Eastern religionist glorifies death: "My friend, welcome the joy of impersonal Nothingness — 'Nothing, this is the end, the Supreme Goal'" (Katha Upanishad 1:3:10). They all leave us hungry again. Where is the answer to the dilemma of our own personal death? Who cares if the world is supposedly going to be a better place someday? What about Number One?

The occultist holds death to be full of great promise and power, a step upward. But again, the promises sound good but leave us confused and unsatisfied. These latest views on death are not fundamentally different from those men have held for ages. Some sort of life after death has always been talked about.

But the Bible promises ''Salvation;'' precisely, salvation from death.

WHY DO WE DIE?

To begin with the Bible supplies the reason why we die. And that's comforting to know.

We die because we sin. That's the basic reason for death. Anyone who sins dies. Jesus Christ did not sin and so He is alive. But the rest of us sin and so we shall die.

What Eve got from the serpent was death. He promised her knowledge and he gave her knowledge, but the sin involved — disobeying God and eating the fruit — resulted in death, something the serpent failed to mention in the original proposition. When we sin we die.

On the face of it it sounds like a harsh judgment by a hard-to-please God. But God established death so that man would not go on living forever in sin (Gen. 3:22). God established death so that man might have the chance to be perfect again, as he was originally made. By having faith in God during life, man attains perfection in death.

So the Bible says something which agrees in part with the white-wash philosophies about death. Death *can* be a step upward. But the all-important factor is the faith in God. God requires true faith for perfection in death.

Now the Fall was genetic. Once our original parents of the Garden of Eden sinned, we all followed suit. The scriptures attest:

Therefore, just as through one man sin entered into the world, and death through sin, and so death spread to all men, because all sinned (Rom. 5:12 NAS).

But the Bible divides death into two parts. There are two different *kinds* of death. *Physical death* is the permanent separation of the human spirit from its body. But *spiritual death* is the permanent separation of the spirit from *God*. It is this second death which is really to be feared.

Living men are now in a state of spiritual death, according to the Bible. Men are now separated from God; they are dead while they live. (See 1 Tim. 5:6; Rev. 3:1; Luke 15:24, 32.) Jesus referred to "The dead burying their own dead," frankly stating that the living human beings around Him were, so far as God was concerned, dead (Luke 9:60 KJV).

Without God, we are the living dead.

SO GREAT A SALVATION

God prepared a solution to the dilemma of death for sinful men which the scriptures refer to as "So great a salvation."

God actually had a problem when man first sinned. God must be just. He could not live with evil or He just wouldn't be a holy God. And having created man how could he eliminate him by death? Do we kill our children if they behave wrongly?

God must be both just and merciful. He must punish sin but he must forgive men. How could He manage both?

Now, we may well say, "What's the problem?" If He were really a kind and decent God, He would just forgive everybody right off. But consider the following:

"There is no reason to equate the divine Fatherhood with softness. How like us it is to get a smug, warm feeling when we think about

God; the feeling which a child has when he is sure that he can get away with almost anything. Such a child may call his lenient father *loving*, but in his heart he knows better. He is conscious that there is something wrong with a paternal love which is so superficial that it makes no demands and warns of no consequences. It is impossible to respect such a father, much less to love him, when it is apparent that he is either too weak or too unconcerned to discipline or punish. Man not only takes advantage of such a God; he inwardly despises him. Nothing less than a divine Being who keeps love and judgment — including punishment — in proper balance is deserving of the name 'Father'."[1] (See Psalm 85:10; James 2:13; Isaiah 45:21; Romans 3:26).

How did God balance "love and judgment"?

He sacrificed Jesus Christ.

The Savior was sinless but He was killed in our place. He was punished for the sins that are really ours.

"I came to give my life a ransom for many" the Lord said. "O foolish men and slow of heart to believe...was it not necessary for the Christ to suffer?"

Paul attested to God's plan to punish His own Son for our death-meriting sins, in order that we might reach perfection: "He made Him who knew no sin to be sin on our behalf, that we might become the righteousness of God in Him" (2 Cor. 5:21 NAS).

Finally, the mighty verse in John 3:16 NAS: "For God so loved the world that He gave His only begotten Son that whosoever believes in Him should not perish but have eternal life."

Each man believing in Christ is saved, "born again" (Acts 16:31). He receives true life after death, or in biblical terms, eternal life.

What actually happens, of course, is that the believer's state of spiritual death is canceled when he receives Christ. There is no longer any possibility of his suffering the second death. He will instead join God forever at the point of his physical death. This is the very essence of the term "saved."

It should be noted — it is vital, in fact — that the system is *conditional*. Men must come to belief in the atoning mission of Jesus Christ or they cannot participate in God's plan. God's mercy is useless to us unless we subscribe to His justice. Merely living "like Christ," obeying the "principles of Christ," doing good works like Christ did, and all the rest of the well-meaning formulas of unsaved men will just get us a permanent separation from God. It's faith — the trust in Christ's provision — which saves us. Obviously, if we don't meet the conditions we shall not obtain the results.

And that's the part left out by the new life-after-death tales, as well as by all the other worldly religions. The belief in our Savior is *not* given as a condition for obtaining mercy in those circles. In fact, Jesus is cast time and again as just one character in the pleasant scenarios from the next world, always graciously accepting and forgiving. The Being of Light requires nothing of us. God is just totally reachable by anyone who can achieve dying. Our sins are of no concern to Him.

They leave out the vital part, the part that really matters. And how it matters! It's truly a matter of life and death!

PEACE WITH GOD

Why does God place such emphasis upon the death of Christ? Can't we just be good people, like He was, and make it on our own merits? After all, if we're really good then we should certainly have the privilege of living forever. If God can defeat death and perfect us later on, why is the death of His Son so important?

A doctrine known as "Imputation" enters the picture at this point. Only righteous people encounter God, according to the scriptures, and the righteousness of

Christ is *imputed* (freely given) to those who simply *believe* in Him. (Rom. 4:6; Rom. 10:3; Phil. 3:9). Human merit does not enter the picture.

Now this is disagreeable to the human sense of pride and accomplishment. If I give charity, conduct an orderly and righteous life and truly carry forth the message of the gospel, insofar as loving my neighbor and forgiving my fellowman his shortcomings, then can't I expect God to be reasonably impressed? Why should I have to die the second death and be forever separated from God if I'm basically a good person?

This question has been asked from time immemorial and the answer is that there are no good people. The Bible gives God's standard for goodness, and only Jesus accomplished it. People teaching "goodness and heavenly light" phrases, rather like the occultists who report from the "next world," are not really good at all in God's sight. People helping other people to die a comfortable death via the practice of OBE are not really helping them at all. In a way they're condemning those people since they're selling them a false gospel, an erroneous way of reaching God, right on their deathbeds.

God's standards are high. He calls man's best works "filthy rags." (Isa. 64:6 KJV) Nobody is holy and that's all there is to that. And if we really think about it, we're never 100% righteous in this life; we never tell the whole truth and we never forgive anyone completely. God may hold to a high standard but He's only being realistic. If God is indeed completely holy, then He wants to spend eternity only with those who are completely holy. And thus we need the righteousness of Christ to make it.

The believer in Christ actually gets a *feeling* of righteousness — a new awakening. Truly, he is reborn. He won't be perfected until the coming of the King, but he feels relocated into God's way. To our knowledge, that feeling is better and more reliable than all the testimonies of mediums, parapsychologists and fascinated M.D.'s who hunger for the life-after-death stories.

Paul speaks of the joy of the man "to whom God reckons righteousness apart from works," (Romans 4:6

NAS) or the joy attending the fact that God is waiting for us despite our lacking character, accomplishment, and merit. This is a view of death that really enhances one's life. There is a future to belief in Christ, to say the least.

If, however, we do not want to believe in the atoning work of Christ, we are stuck with submitting our own good works to God to qualify for eternal life. We are saying that we are good enough to live with God on our own merits, and this is tantamount to saying that God went to unnecessary trouble to punish His Son.

Christ did not have to come at all, of course, if we were good enough to make it on our own. If we had enough righteousness to offer God to begin with, then we wouldn't need any more imputed to us, from whatever source. But that is not the biblical picture of life and death. The Bible says that we must trust in Christ to receive salvation.

The gospel, speaking directly to the matter of life and death, states clearly:

> He that believeth on the Son hath everlasting life: and he that believeth not the Son shall not see life; but the wrath of God abideth on him (Jn. 3:36 KJV).

THE RESURRECTION

The resurrection of Jesus Christ makes the point more plainly than all the scriptures in the Bible. Jesus is the example of what happens to all who believe. This truly is life after death. This is the best case of life after death we know about.

Like Paul we rest our entire case on the resurrection: "…and if Christ has not been raised, your faith is worthless, you are still in your sins…If we have only hoped in Christ *in this life*, we are of all men most to be pitied" (1 Cor. 15:17,19 NAS; emphasis ours).

Biblical believers count on Christ and His resurrection not only in this life but in the life to come — the life after death. That Christ is alive and effective now is more than merely a matter of faith to those who follow Him. Actually the evidence for the resurrection is very convincing. The New Testament is a hazardous book to doubt.

Detractors question the resurrection on the basis that it was originally reported by believers, the Lord's own disciples. They had every reason to exaggerate the impact of Jesus' ministry and so they fabricated this life-after-death story. But a careful reading of the account shows the disciples themselves to be skeptics. The gospel frankly reports the doubting of Thomas, who insisted on examining the wounds of the resurrected Savior personally (Jn. 20:24-31). When Mary reported that she had actually seen the risen Lord, the incredulous disciples "believed not" (Mark 16:11 KJV).

Furthermore, it is unreasonable to suppose that those initial believers, inspired recorders of the deathless Sermon on the Mount and eyewitness to the magnificent miracles of the Lord, would stretch a point to that degree. Did the work of Jesus Christ really need help? Would the world have simply discounted all that He said and did if he were not raised from the dead? Actually, the devotion of the disciples and their faith in the resurrection is more than proved by their ongoing work for the gospel. They were beaten, starved and finally martyred in their efforts to take the Word of God to the world. One would think that at the point where Peter was to be crucified upside down, dying a slow and agonizing death, he would have renounced the resurrection, knowing it to be a fake anyway. It's very hard to believe that men would die for a mere invention of their own minds.

And then no body was ever produced. One would think that the skeptics, and there were many, would have simply paraded the corpse of the Lord through the streets to put the resurrection story to rest once and for all. They went to special pains to guard the body; certainly they would have gone to some trouble to display it. But only if they had it. Instead, they kept very quiet indeed, as the Lord continued His ministry for forty days.

And as to the New Testament in general, it has been examined by experts, believing and unbelieving, and it has stood up to all tests. Most historians would agree that if the stringent validity tests applied to these documents were applied to all history, any number of worthy personalities — Plato, the Caesars, Alexander, etc. — and important events would fade into myth. The New Testament stands up to any historical account as to its veracity, and nearly 2,000 years of doubting inquiry has failed to invalidate a single page. The Old Testament does as well but cannot be tested as vigorously, being so much more ancient. Again, however, no archaeological, historical, scientific discovery or comparison with other valid accounts has ever turned up an undisputed error in the Old Testament either. (*The New Testament Documents: Are They Reliable?* by Dr. F. F. Bruce gives a thorough examination of the rigorous testing of the scriptural accounts and their ultimate acceptance by the most skeptical of experimenters.)

Lawyers, among others, have looked into the New Testament in an objective way, regarding it as they would any testimony in a courtroom. Simon Greenleaf, Royall Professor of Law at Harvard, whose 1842 masterpiece, *A Treatise on the Law of Evidence* "is still considered the greatest single authority on evidence in the entire literature of legal procedure,"[2] found the New Testament accounts completely trustworthy. He critically examined the documents and the surrounding facts and circumstances of the times. Finally evaluating the New Testament authors, he concluded with "an undoubting conviction of their integrity, ability, and truth."[3] "We did not follow cleverly devised tales...but we were eyewitnesses," Peter testifies (2 Pet. 1:16 KJV).

Naturally, believers tend to subscribe to the resurrection out of pure faith. But even neutral parties who have tested the New Testament come out with the highest regard for the reportage, including the reportage about the resurrection. We submit now the commentary of a few examiners of unquestionable scholarly repute in regard to the resurrection:

Thomas Arnold (appointed to the chair of Modern History at Oxford, author of the famous three volume *History of Rome*:

> "...I know of no one fact in the history of mankind which is proved by better and fuller evidence of every sort." [4]

Lord Darling (a former Lord Chief Justice of England):

> "In its favor as a living truth, there exists such overwhelming evidence, positive and negative, factual and circumstantial, that no intelligent jury in the world could fail to bring in a verdict that the resurrection story is true." [5]

John Singleton Copley (Lord Lyndhurst, recognized as one of the greatest legal minds in British history, Solicitor General of the British government, Attorney General of Great Britain, three times High Chancellor of England, elected High Steward of Cambridge):

> "I know pretty well what evidence is; and I tell you such evidence as that for the Resurrection has never broken down yet." [6]

Sir Edward Clarke, K.C.:

> "As a lawyer, I have made a prolonged study of the evidences for the events of the first Easter Day. To me, the evidence is conclusive, and over and over again in the High Court I have secured the verdict on evidence not nearly so compelling." [7]

Purely secular reference sources also tend to support the validity of the resurrection. Accepted non-Christian reference works (e.g. *The World's Great Religions*, Time Inc. and many others) speak in terms of the resurrection being firmly based on actual events. The amount of books published on the ministry, death and new life of Christ is staggering; in this supposedly secular age people are vitally interested in this particular version of life after death; "...in the past century alone, 60,000 books have sought to explain Christ." [8]

Of course many books try to discount the resurrection, advancing other possibilities and rather arcane theories about how such a thing could even be reported. Most popular among these are the swoon theory, where the Lord didn't really die at all; the theft theory, where someone stole the body and invented the story; the hallucination theory, where all those who saw the Lord after the resurrection were deluded; the mistaken identity theory, where it was someone else who approached the disciples and continued the teaching of Jesus Christ; and the wrong grave theory, where neither the friends nor enemies of Christ could remember where he had been buried three days before. We leave the reader to evaluate those without further comment.

It is beyond our scope here to consider all of the pro and con ideas advanced through the ages about the resurrection, but we do, of course, want to present it as a reported life-after-death experience. An endless stream of commentaries is available to the seeker, but the reader is forewarned that people examining the resurrection tend to come to belief in Christ. The stories are legion of religious conversions on the part of even hardened atheists who first set out to discount the resurrection. We would refer the reader particularly to Josh McDowell's two-volume *Evidence That Demands A Verdict* [9] compiled by a former skeptic, which is probably the most complete modern commentary on the historical evidence for the truth of Christianity, including the resurrection.

The Book of Acts wraps up the idea of judgment and the function of the resurrection in the affairs of men succinctly:

> Therefore, having overlooked the times of ignorance, God is now declaring to men that all everywhere should repent, because He has

fixed a day in which He will judge the world in righteousness through a Man (Jesus) whom He has appointed, having furnished proof to all men by raising Him from the dead. (17:30-31 NAS)

ON TO BETTER THINGS

So much for the Biblical theory of death. God's view is available in more-printings than any other life-after-death work, and we can only refer the reader to the Bible for the whole story. We will now turn to the Biblical view of the next life. We will see that the Lord comments at length about eternal life and even discusses the present condition of those who have already died.

1. Leslie Woodson, *Hell and Salvation*, (Old Tappan, N.J.: Fleming H. Revell Co.) 1973, p. 66-7, used by permission.
2. Simon Greenleaf, *Testimony of the Evangelists, Examined by the Rules of Evidence Administered in Courts of Justice*, (Grand Rapids: Baker) 1965, p. 46 (1847 reprint) and Wilbur M. Smith, *Therefore Stand* (Grand Rapids: Baker) 1972, p. 423-5.
3. Ibid.
4. Smith p. 426 citing T. Arnold, *Sermons on the Christian Life*, 6th ed., London 1859, p. 324.
5. Michael Green, *Man Alive* (Chicago: InterVarsity) 1969, p. 54.
6. Wilbur Smith, *Therefore Stand*, p. 425, 584.
7. John Stott, *Basic Christianity*, (1971), p. 47.
8. *Time*, June 21, 1971.
9. Campus Crusade For Christ, Arrowhead Springs, San Bernardino, Calif.

We are engulfed in an occult explosion which has been predicted to immediately precede the return of Christ. Paramount among these prophecies is the warning about an awesome acceleration of demonic deception.

I believe that Weldon and Levitt's book unveils an upsurge of a very old and insidiously appealing deception which has surfaced at various times in history. I refer to the idea that the dead are free to roam around as spirits and communicate "superior" wisdom to the living. The "after-death" experience as chronicled by Drs. Moody, Kubler-Ross and others is but a variation of this theme.

That this phenomena is occurring among unbelievers in near-death states is simply an indication of the level of subtlety that spiritual warfare can assume.

However, the dead are not able to roam freely. Scripture is clear that the unsaved dead are confined and that the saved are with Christ.

We must not place our trust in experiences, but in God's word. For those who have not placed their trust in Christ, death is not the welcome friend these experiences would have us believe, but is something to be greatly feared.

Hal Lindsey

"Inasmuch as it is appointed for men to die once, and after this comes judgment."

Hebrews 9:27 NAS

8

God and Death

According to the Bible everyone will experience life after death. The question is not whether an individual will enter eternity, but *where* he will spend it.

The Bible discusses death practically. It shows the way to prepare for it and it tells about the life that follows.

Comparing for a moment the Biblical life after death with the occult views of life after death we find them utterly opposed. The Bible, as we will show, indicates that the dead may not be contacted and that no one living may go into the "next world" to check out death (or at least it must always be a one-way trip). Those who died formerly in unbelief are confined, as we will see, and those who died believing we shall encounter only later on. Consulting mediums to attempt communication with the dead is expressly prohibited in the Bible:

> Do not turn to mediums or spiritists; do not seek them out to be defiled by them. I am the Lord your God (Lev. 19:31 NAS).

> Should not a people consult their God? Should
> they (instead) consult the dead on behalf of the
> living? (Isa. 8:19 NAS)

But people have always been fascinated with the possibility of consulting the dead despite God's admonitions. So zealous an Israelite as King Saul consulted a medium with drastic results (see 1 Sam. 28): "So Saul died for his trespass which he committed against the Lord, because of the word of the Lord which he did not keep, and also because he asked counsel of a medium, making inquiry of it, and did not inquire of the Lord. Therefore He killed him...(1 Chr. 10:13-14 NAS).

Apparently contact with the dead is God's province exclusively. We feel tht the contactees of the mediums are demonic because, according to the scriptures, they cannot be the actual dead. We also feel that the Biblical admonition against such exercises ought to be taken seriously.

Instead, the Bible says we are to take the Word of God at face value and count on the sacrifice of Christ to take us into eternal life. Any inquiry we may have on behalf of the dead can be answered through prophecy and the Biblical passages which account for the disposition of all souls who ever lived.

But an exaggerated interest in death is an unhealthy and unspiritual endeavor, anyway. Demons are always associated with graveyards and our "horror" literature and movies present the "living dead" as a staple product, whether in the form of zombies and vampires or just the wailing ghosts of bygone eras. Jesus observed, "Wherever the corpse is, there the vultures will gather" (Mt. 24:28 NAS). A belief that evil spirits lurk about the dead is common in India, China and among many primitive peoples. Various societies had rituals to keep the spirits away from the dead; American Indians fired arrows into the air, and the Chinese used firecrackers (which probably kept the living away as well).

Death holds a certain revulsion for the living person, and this is natural. A desire to encounter it before one's time is a perversion of something natural.

WE SHALL NOT ALL SLEEP

Believers are naturally concerned about death and are supplied with the normal preservation of life instinct. While the faith promises eternal life the believer still loves life in the here and now. While he counts on going to be with the Lord in death he still wants to live, serving the Lord, in this present existence.

Not all believers will die, the Bible says. Actually quite a few will be alive when the Lord returns — millions of them. These will be directly translated to heaven, their bodies changed and outfitted for eternal life:

> Behold, I shew you a mystery; We shall not all sleep (in death), but we shall all be changed, in a moment, in the twinkling of an eye, at the last trump: for the trumpet shall sound, and the dead shall be raised incorruptible, and we shall be changed. For this corruptible (flesh) must put on incorruption, and this mortal (body) must put on immortality (1 Cor. 15:51-53 KJV).

So there is a chance — there has always been a chance — for the believer in Christ to *avoid death altogether!* As Enoch and Elijah were directly translated to heaven while still living, the believers expect to be taken in what is known as the "Rapture" — the translation of the Church to heaven. All souls who ever believed throughout the age of the church will be translated in the Rapture, but "The dead in Christ shall rise first: Then we which are alive and remain shall be caught up together with them in the clouds, to meet the Lord in the air: and so shall we ever be with the Lord" (I Thess. 4:16-17 KJV).

Hence the Lord said, "I go to prepare a place for you" (Jn. 14:2 KJV). And so Paul sang:

O death, where is thy sting? O grave, where is thy victory? (I Cor. 15:55 KJV)

"THE RESURRECTION AND THE LIFE"

The near-death experience of a Christian believer which we will now present greatly differs from the reports given earlier in the secular research. At this point we need to re-emphasize that, believer or non-believer, these experiences are the exception, not the rule.

Betty Malz had been in a coma for 44 days, hovering between life and death.[1] At the time she had the following experience the resuscitation instruments had already been disconnected and a sheet pulled over her face. She was assumed dead. Her father knelt by her bedside in prayer.

But the patient was aware of her father's prayer; "All he could say was 'Jesus, Jesus!'" she reports. Her story continues:

> As he was saying this, I was approaching a beautiful hill. To the right of me was a silvery marble wall. At the top of the hill were gates of pearl. I heard resounding voices of worship an angelic chorus singing, "Glory to the name of Jesus." I joined the singing.
>
> The angel to the left of me asked, "Would you like to go in and join the chorus?"
>
> "No," I answered. "I would like to sing for a while, and then I'd like to go back to my family."
>
> He nodded. I turned around and went back down the hill, and as I went the sun was rising over the beautiful marble wall.
>
> In my room the early morning sun rays were pouring through the clear window over the air conditioner near my bed. Often, I have seen dust particles dancing in sun rays. But as I

looked at these rays slanting across my bed, I could see ivory letters about two inches high go before my vision like a stock market tape report. And these were the words: St. John 11:25——'' I am the resurrection and the life: he that believeth in me, though he were dead, yet shall he live.''

I reached out in wonder to take hold of these words of God. In doing so, I pushed back the sheet covering me and touched those words with my hand. When I did this, life came into my fingers, through my arms and all through my body — and I pushed back the sheet and sat up. No man can take credit for my healing, the Word of God healed me.

My father was simply overwhelmed. Although he had seen God heal people in answer to prayer during his ministry, he had never seen anything like this!

The nurse's aide who had been attending me and was in the room at the time went into immediate action. She ran out of the room screaming, ''It's a ghost!''

And no one could get her to come back in during the 48 hours following that I was still in the hospital.

Doctors, nurses, newspapermen, a Catholic priest, and some sisters began coming into my room to ask me all about it. It was a joy for me to share with them what had happened and to give testimony for my Lord.

That remarkable experience served to enhance the faith of the subject considerably. Very much alive today, she says, ''Now I know the joy of living and testifying for Jesus and praising His name. Now I truly appreciate the privilege of knowing Christ personally and serving Him.''

So the first difference between the above testimony and the life-after-death experiences reported in the secular research is the difference in the reaction by the subject. Mrs. Malz now continues in her faith, her walk with the Lord enhanced and her doctrine and beliefs in no way changed. This is a far cry from the reassuring but questionable, "Now I know we have nothing to worry about. Everyone is accepted after death." The latter of course contradicts the Bible, not to mention the moral reckoning of any number of non-biblical civilizations. As we said earlier it seems to represent an example of demonic activity meant to lead men astray.

Mrs. Malz's experience had no hint of judgment — not even a "review" of her life followed by the rubber-stamp acceptance. There is no judgment in the case of a believer since Christ was already punished on the believer's behalf. (Romans 8:1)

There were no earthly characters in Mrs. Malz's experience — no "living dead" to assist her passage. There was no Being of Light, but the Lord's presence was indicated by the song of praise. The experience contained highly relevant scriptural commentary for Mrs. Malz to understand and profit by, and obviously she has.

Now of course, we would be advocating a double standard if we said that Mrs. Malz died and came back to life and the secular folks were only fooled by demons. In fact, we must continue with our contention that no one who is alive was ever dead, including Mrs. Malz. It is the *kind* or *quality* of experience we wish to emphasize in this case. Unbelievers seem to experience false doctrine of a kind specifically attributed to Satan in the Bible; believers (and there are other similar cases) experience doctrinally accurate events, which might come right out of the scriptures. We *would* expect the presence of angels, songs of praise and lessons in scripture in the hereafter, to take the Bible at face value. All of these are replete throughout the Book of Revelation in its heavenly scenes. And we *would* expect the utter absence of all of those things, or some crude masquerades, in the case of unbelievers. That is, Biblically, the way things are.

WHERE ARE THE DEAD?

A lot of people have died. Where are they?

The Bible speaks to that very plainly. And it divides all past mankind into two large groups — the saved and the unsaved. Salvation, as we said, refers explicitly to death; from death we are saved, to go to eternal life. Some say we are saved from sin but they mean the same thing ("The wages of sin is death"). Sin means separation from God and those who die in sin, unsaved, will be away from the presence of God forever, according to the scriptures. Those whose sins are forgiven, via the payment made by Jesus Christ, are reconciled to God and thus defeat death.

The Bible comments at length about the position of the *saved* dead. They go to be with the Lord:

> For to me to live is Christ and to die is gain...
> having a desire to depart and to be with Christ,
> which is far better (Phil. 1:21, 23 KJV)

The apostle considers departing to be with Christ as "far better" than remaining alive. Death is "gain" to Paul, since he anticipates the very presence of the Lord.

In Luke 23:43 NAS, the Lord Himself clearly indicates that the saved dead join Him. He tells the repentant thief on the cross:

> Truly I say to you, today you shall be with Me
> in paradise.

On other occasions this overwhelming promise issued from the lips of the Lord. In His reassuring Upper Room discourse He told the disciples about His going to prepare a place for them so that "where I am there you may be also" (see Jn. 14:1-3 NAS). Speaking in the context of eternal life He repeated "where I am, there shall My servant also be" (Jn. 12:26 NAS). And He prayed:

> Father, I desire that they also, whom Thou hast
> given Me, be with Me where I am, that they

may behold My glory (My final triumph) (Jn. 17:24 NAS).

Paul wrote to the church at Corinth in terms of his yerning "to be absent from the body and to be at home with the Lord" (2 Cor. 5:8 NAS).

Even those future believers, slain after the Rapture of the church in the coming period of Great Tribulation (see Matt. 24), are seen in prophecy as being with the Lord and speaking to Him (Rev. 6:10 et al).

The martyr Stephen (Acts 7) accused his tormentors of heresy, proved his point from the scriptures and was stoned to death in perfect faith. He had not the vaguest doubt that the Lord would be ready to receive him immediately upon his death and he preached the same with his dying breath, "Lord Jesus receive my spirit," (vv. 55-59 KJV).

This, then, is the joy of the believer. If the scriptures are to be taken seriously, there *is* abundant life after death and it awaits the follower of Christ. The saved dead are undoubtedly with Him in heaven. They will dwell eternally in the presence of God.

Not so, however with the *unsaved dead*, God's second large category of men. The Bible's most unpopular passages deal with the confinement and punishment of those who died, and *will* die, in unbelief. "No decent God would punish human beings," say the humanitarians and religionists who wish to escape the uncomfortable biblical future for unbelievers. "I don't want any God who cannot see how worthy I am." The litany of rebelliousness, begun in the Garden, goes on and on.

But the scriptures are very clear. The Lord sounded enough warnings for the entire human race to hear ("You fool, this very night your soul is required of you!" — Luke 12:20 NAS). Jesus told his disciples that they need not fear killers among men, "who kill the body, and after that have no more that they can do." Those killers only cause the first death, the physical death. They are fearful enough, of course, but the Lord's point was to warn of the wrath of a righteous God, Who has sway over the final death: "Fear the One who after He has killed has authority *to cast into hell*; yes, I tell you, *fear Him!*" (Luke 12:4-5 NAS).

Curiously, some people who swear by the passages on heaven in the Bible utterly reject the passages on hell, and obviously this is not rational. The vast majority of our clinical death reports were replete with quasi-heavenly scenes, but missing were the signs of the other side of things. No judgments, no troubles, nothing but pure acceptance awaits us all, according to those reports. But it seems obvious that the "heavenly" parts of those scenarios were drawn from the scriptural ideal. What represented all the scriptures which frankly report on hell? If the Bible contains both, how did those reports get so selective?

Apparently we experience what we *want* to experience, and we censor out what might make us unhappy. We can actually kid ourselves to hell, as it were.

Hell is described in the Bible in a variety of terms: "outer darkness," "the resurrection of judgment," "the black darkness," "the punishment of eternal fire," "the place where there is weeping and gnashing of teeth," "eternal punishment," etc.[2] But why would it have to be described as eternal? Probably because no amount of punishment *in time* has any *meaning* when compared to the *eternity* of eternity, and because without the punishment of evil, there is no justice. In eternity, there *is* no time, hence, if in eternity there is to be any justice — any punishment of evil — it must last forever, or else be ultimately meaningless. The problem is not that hell exists — it must exist if God is infinitely holy and any distinction is to be made between good and evil. A Hitler or Stalin must not go unpunished. The problem is that men do not understand how *evil* sin is when compared to a Being who is *truly* infinitely holy — that the smallest sin is justly worthy of eternal punishment. Since God is infinitely just, the eternal punishment of sin can be no more or less severe — or just — than that which is demanded by the case. If hell is real, and it is, remember also:

119

> God is not wishing for any to perish, but for all
> to come to repentance. He desires all men to be
> saved and to come to the knowledge of the
> truth. (2 Peter 3:9; I Tim. 2:4 NAS).

and,

> For God so loved the world that He gave His
> only begotten Son that whosoever believeth in
> Him should not perish but have everlasting
> life. (John 3:16 KJV)

If the Son of God Himself had to die a horribly
torturous death, and had to have the judgment of all
men's sins *placed on Him* simply to allow for the
possibility of man's salvation, we must not think God will
go lightly with those who act as if He doesn't even care.

A number of verses in the Bible refer to a specific place
of confinement for the unsaved dead.[3] Jesus spoke of a
hypocrite whose faith in his master was not real: "The
Master of that slave will come on a day when he does not
expect him...and assign him a *place* with the
unbelievers" (Lk. 12:46-7 NAS). The rich man wanted
to warn his brothers lest they come "to this place of
torment" (Lk. 16:28 NAS). The betrayer Judas "went to
his own place" (Acts 1:25 NAS).

The Epistles of Peter are conclusive in this regard.
Through First and Second Peter the apostle refers to the
disobedient spirits "now in prison" (1 Peter 3:19; 4:6
NAS) and the sinning angels being committed by God to
"pits of darkness reserved for judgment." Peter
concludes:

> The Lord knows how to rescue the godly from
> temptation, and to keep the unrighteous *under
> punishment* for the day of judgment (2 Pet.
> 2:9 NAS).

Without wishing to sound like "hellfire and
damnation" preachers, we must still elucidate these

verses so relevant to our discussion. It's a highly metaphysical or spiritual point, but if the *unsaved dead* are confined and the *saved dead* are with Christ, then no one has seen any dead person, except perhaps in rare circumstances where God permits it with believers as in the case of Samuel.

We could discuss at length the impossibility of valid communication with the unsaved dead in the Biblical view. They are simply not reachable. That situation would upset God's doctrine on life and death entirely. This is not to say, of course, that demon activity could not result in a deception; if we are subject to occultic experiences, we may experience just about anything the devil can dream up to divert us. But it does go to say that the Bible knows of no going and coming between life and death. If in Luke 16, the unsaved dead could not even cross over to the realm of the saved, it seems clear they cannot "come over" to the living.

Dr. Merrill Unger's definitive *Bible Dictionary* sums up:

> The blessed dead being with Abraham were conscious and "comforted" (Luke 16:25). The dying thief was on that very day to be with Christ in "Paradise." The unsaved were separated from the saved by a "great gulf fixed" (Luke 16:26). The rich man, who is evidently still in Hades, is a representative case and describes the unjudged condition in the intermediate state of the wicked. As to his spirit, he was alive, fully conscious and in exercise of his mental faculties and also tormented. It is thus apparent that insofar as the unsaved dead are concerned, no change in their abode or state is revealed in connection with the ascension of Christ. At the sinners' judgment of the Great White Throne, Hades will surrender the wicked. They will be judged and be cast into the Lake of Fire (Rev. 20:13, 14).

That the human spirit continues to exist consciously after the death of the body is a fact most clearly established upon a biblical basis; to say nothing of the strength of philosophical arguments upon the matter. That a most powerful contrast is declared between the state of the righteous and that of the wicked, not only after the final judgment, but also during the interval between that event and the death of the body should also be regarded as beyond question. [4]

Thus there are but two kinds of men, whether one considers past, present or future. Those who believe in God and His plan of salvation through the vicarious sacrifice of Jesus Christ have one expectation, and those who don't have the other. The people who died before us are accounted in one of the two groups and those who come after us fall under the same economy. And finally, all of those alive now may choose, as all men have chosen, their group. The way of salvation is, of course, always open to all men.

The people already dead are out of our reach completely. The Bible speaks of no "visitation" possibility. The Bible cannot conceivably be reconciled to any life-after-death experience reported by a living individual. Life after death, in the Biblical view, is possible for any person, but it is obtained through the principles of the gospel of Christ and never by any human preparation, acts of merit or scientific phenomena.

God awards eternal life on the basis of faith.

HELL ON EARTH

Hell is not really so hard to imagine. We just have to look at what's going on among us now.

"How can there be a hell?" is one of the unbiblical person's constant questions. Nobody likes the idea of hell, least not of all God, Who has gone to some real trouble to preserve and sanctify His children. But we have some very real intimations of hell on the earth right now, in our daily papers.

Hell must be a place where the most evil thoughts of a vast community of men gain free reign. Hell must be a place where all the Hitlers and Stalins who have ever lived compete for power (for not just those demigods, but all of us who would, given the chance, act as they did!). Hell must be where there is no further alternative — where the war is never over, the frustration never eased, the prayer always hopeless.

Theologians — serious Bible scholars — have wrestled with the matter of hell for ages. The true Bible believer is not proud or conceited in his gift of salvation (Eph. 2:8-9) but rather very humbled. It is obvious at least up to this point in history that a majority of men will not qualify under God's plan of salvation as matters stand, and that's troubling. The Lord commanded us to "love all men," and believers cannot be satisfied with the worldly situation.

This is an awful world, presently. No matter what is said about our plight today by optimistic scientists, false religionists or the occultists who see better things ahead after death, this is an awful world. And this awful world bodes nothing but more awfulness for the future.

People are starving and no one feeds them. People are oppressed and other people sell them out for political gain. The military forces in the world may blow the whole place up at any time and we all know it. Most thinking people would not be at all surprised by the arrival of a nuclear war that will reduce this planet and all it contains to poisoned rubble. The Armageddon of the Bible, that final holocaust, seems too near, too much on our present agenda.

How can God sit through all this? Why doesn't He do something?

Well, of course, He *has* done something. Who could do more than "lay down His life for His friends"?

Modern theologians have had some interesting thoughts on the cosmic question, "Why hell?"

123

Understandably moved by the human condition and the chaos of today's world they have struggled with the nature of God, His expressed will in the scriptures and the outcome of His plans for men.

They have advanced some very interesting ideas:

> "The nature of God is justice to balance His love. The fact that God's time of patience will end and He will strike out in justice is the hope of the sin-cursed universe. If God does not act to destroy, then we face an eternity of sinfulness. But God is holy and just, and therefore He will destroy. For believers, He has already moved to destroy their sin by placing it on Christ and dealing with it for eternity, but upon those who will not enter into Christ, the flood of His wrath must fall. Hell is as much a part of the love story of God as heaven.[5]

> Men are pleased to receive the Bible revelation concerning Heaven, but do not heed its warning regarding hell. Human sentiment, opinion, and reasons are valueless concerning these eternal issues. It is wisdom to heed the voice of the Son of God, and He more than any other has stressed the woes of the lost (Matt. 5:22, 29 30; 10:28; 18:9; 23:15, 33; Mark 9:43, 47; Luke 12:5). If eternal punishment cannot be comprehended, it should be remembered that infinite holiness and the sin by which infinite holiness is outraged are equally unmeasurable by the human mind. God is not revealed as one who causes good people to suffer in hell; but He is revealed as one who at infinite cost has wrought to the end that sinners, believing in Christ, may not perish, but have everlasting life."[6]

Harold O. Brown has said "Hell has been called 'the most enduring monument to the freedom of the human will'", and C. S. Lewis stated: "There are only two kinds of people in the end: Those who say to God 'Thy will be done', and those to whom God says, in the end, *'Thy* will be done.' " [7]

Lewis expanded on this idea:

> If a game is played, it must be possible to lose it. If the happiness of a creature lies in self-surrender, no one can make that surrender but himself (though many can help him to make it) and he may refuse. I would pay any price to be able to say truthfully 'All will be saved.' But my reason retorts, 'Without their will, or with it?' If I say, 'without their will' I at once perceive a contradiction; how can the supreme voluntary act of self-surrender be involuntary? If I say 'With their will,' my reason replies 'How if they *will not* give in?' [8]

And that final quotation is the real hell about hell — that we choose it for ourselves. It is not God, in truth, who chooses hell for us, but we ourselves. We can choose it in life, in effect, (and we see the world choosing it everyday), and we can choose it in death.

We know of no other authority than the Bible in the discussion of life after death. We have given, throughout this book, the various views as we find them today, including the latest sensational clinical reports. But we find them wanting compared to the timeless, relevant message of the Word of God. We have, accurately and patiently, we hope, given the statistics and the sources, and we have tried to trace man's latest ideas about his most engaging and troubling question — where he's really going when he dies. But we have more or less come home again — back to the Bible.

We just don't trust those reports and we've given our reasons. We certainly would never gamble with the message of salvation and how it is obtained in God's will. We would not take a chance on hell for anything. We would not take the new courses in how to pass smoothly over into death for fear of offending the Creator of life, and we think that stands to reason.

At this point we should like to summarize and pull together our discussion. What are our conclusions to date?

In certain cases where reasonable evidence exists, the out-of-the-body experiences may be real. For example, when a revived patient, who was unconscious, describes the doctors actions in accurate detail. It is also at least possible that the experience, or most of them, could be totally in the brain. However, the realm of reality and unreality is by no means easily distinguished once demonic influences enter the picture. A demonic capacity clearly exists to manipulate a person's mental state to such a degree that the unreal illusion becomes experienced as totally real.

If the experiences are real, however, it is crucial to recognize they do *not* represent the totality of what really happens at death. The use of real experiences which validate a false world view has always been a key tactic of the enemy. In the clinical-death phenomena — although the experience, or at least parts of it, may be real enough — the interpretation placed upon it (e.g., there is nothing to fear in death) is false.

A simple half-minute out-of-the-body experience in and of itself would not necessarily remove the fear of death with the degree of conviction as represented in the clinical death cases. However, it is another story when they occur *in near death states*, and when *dead friends and relatives* are seen in perfect health and contentment, and when a "being of light" emanating great love and joy appears with a comforting message. These additional elements of the experience cause the conviction that death is a "friend," a friend who represents the transition to greater happiness, instead of an enemy who brings eternal judgment.

Whether or not an OBE, assuming it is real, is of God or Satan depends on whether the experience itself, and its impact, is biblical or not. Obviously, religious but non-biblical messages from a "being of light" or "the dead" are not of God. This isn't to say that Christians, in rare circumstances may not have OBEs in the near-death state. When we die, the spirit does leave the body (Ecc. 12:7; Luke 8:55; I Kings 17:21-23). God is sovereign and can do as He pleases. God may reveal part of the spirit realm if it suits his purposes, as He did with Paul and Elisha (2 Cor 12; 2 Kings 6:17. These experiences were, however, of a different nature than the clinical death ones.) Paul also states he didn't *know* if he was in the body or not i.e., he couldn't tell — and that he was not permitted to speak about what he did see. This experience is in contrast to those of today. The Christian is to "walk by faith, not by sight."

If a Christian were critically injured in an accident and the process of dying had begun, God might send him back if it was not his time to go. Again, Christian experiences of this type are clearly the exception, not the rule, and by no means should a Christian seek out-of-the-body experiences. A mature Christian will leave things in God's hands. The occultist takes things into his own. And non-believers who are close to death have rejected God up to that point in their lives and cannot logically expect protection from deception in the spirit realm.

It is important to point out here that there is also the possibility of natural mechanisms triggering OBEs; e.g., lack of oxygen, extreme physiological stress, etc. These would not be satanic, although again, once the spirit realm is entered, a person may be subject to its influences. The non-Christian would interpret the experience in light of his world view or in light of how the experience was defined for him, e.g., "death is good." The Christian would interpret the experience in light of his world view, e.g., expecting to see the Lord. Our point is simply that not *all* out-of-the-body experiences, whether Christian or not, are to be accepted uncritically, *as they are reported*.

There could be a variety of other possible explanations, and two people can *interpret* the same experience in different ways. This *interpretation* may or may not be in accordance with the actual facts. What is clear is that because the Christian has the Holy Spirit indwelling him, he is protected in ways the non-Christian is not. Not all OBEs need be satanic. Not all OBEs need be real. If Satan were to operate in enough key cases to provide a significant cultural impact relating to the nature of death, this would be sufficient. However, the few experiences which are reported by Christians are, expectedly, different than those of the non-Christian.

There are common elements, as might be expected from two people entering the same spiritual realm: these include being out of the body, feelings of peace and joy, seeing light all around, etc. However, the *main* part of the experience, and its impact, are different. Christians hear the sound of praise to God and singing. "To be absent from the body and to be present *with* the Lord. (2 Cor. 5:8; Phil. 1:23 KJV) A Christian experience will involve him being with *the Lord*—not with other spirits. We would perhaps grant that other saved Christians may on rare occasion be seen because they too are "with the Lord." However, the result of a Christian's clinical death experience would be that it always brings him *closer to Christ*, and they "come back" more committed to Him than ever. By contrast, non-Christian out-of-the-body clinical death experiences generally take a person further *away* from Christ and salvation, and may end up involving them in the occult.

There are very valid reasons for obeying God and not becoming involved in the occult. As we have seen, occultists often utilize astral projection to travel to other realms. Whereas many of these realms are imaginary, adepts possibly do go out of the body. The spirit realm is real and can possibly be visited temporarily, but the very visit gives one a *false* idea about the next life. They think that what they experience will *be extended forever* at death — when in fact, true death will bring irrevocable judgment.

They also see the dead and may communicate with deceased friends and family, adding to the deception. Once we enter the spirit world *against* God's wishes, we have no guarantee against demonic deception via impersonation of the dead. Thus, the OBE experience is at its core deceptive. Because the spirit realm is so truly beautiful, it is even more appealing and deceptive, especially when it is thought that we will exist there forever regardless of our attitude toward the salvation of Christ.

But the salvation of Christ is what we now wish to discuss.

This book has a happy ending.

We're finished discussing hell and we'd like to now discuss heaven. Happily, the Bible gives a thrilling amount of details on the true life after death.

Eternal life with God is magnificent! The prospect is the happiest thought the human mind can think. Just writing about what's going to happen to those who've chosen God is a wonderfully rejuvenating endeavor.

What's more precious than life?

Eternal Life!

1. Betty Malz, "24 Hours" phamplet, from 705 E. Austin, Pasadena, Texas 77502. See her book *My Glimpse of Eternity* (Texas: Word Inc.)

2. Matthew 3:7-12; 8:12; 22:13; 25:46; Mark 9:43, 48; John 5:29; Rev. 19:20; 20:10, 12, 15, etc.

3. An examination of some of the key Greek scholars and other authorities all unequivocably support the confinement of the unsaved dead — A.T. Robertson, Kenneth Wuest, Kittle, Vincent, etc.

4. Merril Unger, *Unger's Bible Dictionary* (Chicago: Moody Press, Moody Bible Institute) © 1957, p. 61 and 66. Used by permission.

5. Woodson, *Hell and Salvation*, p. 68 citing Donald Barnhouse, *Genesis — A Devotional Exposition I*, (Grand Rapids: Zondervan) © 1970, p. 51-2. Used by permission.

6. Woodson, p. 107 citing L.S. Chaefer, *Major Bible Themes*, Grand Rapids: Zondervan) 1926, p. 298-9.

7. Woodson, p. 70 from *The Protest of a Troubled Protestant*, (New Rochelle, New York: Arlington House) 1969, p. 213; C.S. Lewis, *The Great Divorce* (New York: Macmillan) 1946, p. 69.

8. C.S. Lewis, *The Problem of Pain*, (New York: Macmillan) © 1943, 1971, p. 118-9.

"If a man dies, will he live again? All the days of my struggle I will wait, until my change comes."

Job 14:14 NAS

"Fear not that your life shall come to an end, but rather that it shall never have a beginning."

John Henry Newman

9

Eternity

> The wolf also shall dwell with the lamb, and
> the leopard shall lie down with the kid; and
> the calf and the young lion and the fatling to-
> gether; and a little child shall lead them.

> They shall not hurt nor destroy in all my holy
> mountain: for the earth shall be full of the
> knowledge of the Lord, as the waters cover the
> sea.

So sings the prophet Isaiah about the idyllic conditions
of the future Kingdom of God (11:6,9, KJV). Truly,
God's will shall be done on earth as it is in heaven.

All nature will respond to this marvelous new order.
Even man, the superior killer, will lay down his arms:

> And they shall beat their swords into plow-
> shares and their spears into pruning hooks:
> nation shall not lift up a sword against nation,
> neither shall they learn war anymore (Mic. 4:3,
> KJV).

The above scripture, describing true world peace, is quoted on the facade of the United Nations headquarters in New York City, but without the beginning of the same verse: "And He shall judge among many people, and rebuke strong nations afar off..."

In any case, evil and all its pretenses will be done away within this coming reign of the Lord:

> And I saw an angel coming down from heaven ...and he laid hold of Satan, and bound him a thousand years, and threw him into the abyss and shut it and sealed it over him, so that he should not deceive the nations any longer... (Rev 20:1-3, NAS).

With Satan bound, the earth will be a better place, to say the least. The King will reign in Jerusalem and the believers of all ages will prevail along with Him:

> Do not be afraid, little flock, for your Father has chosen gladly to give you The Kingdom! (Lk. 12:32, NAS)

> Well done, thou good and faithful servant: thou hast been faithful over a few things, I will make thee ruler over many things: enter thou into the joy of thy Lord (Mt. 25:21, KJV).

We will have been changed to immortality by that time (1 Cor. 15:51-53) so that a lifespan will reach 1,000 years and death will be all but abolished:

> For the youth will die at the age of one hundred and the one who does not reach the age of one hundred shall be thought accursed...They shall not labor in vain, or bear children for calamity...(Isa. 65:20,23).

This Kingdom or "millennium" as it is also called in the Bible, will prevail on the earth for 1,000 years.

And then, Eternity!

Looking ahead from where we now stand in God's announced plan, we can see that a number of prophetic events have to take place before we encounter God's final economy, eternity.

Books such as Hal Lindsey's *Late Great Planet Earth* and *Satan in the Sanctuary*, by McCall and Levitt, give actual schedules for the biblical period known as the "end times." No one knows the dates of these upcoming events, but their order is clear in the scriptures. God included in His Word a genuine "word to the wise." Doubting Bible prophecy has proved to be very foolish for very many throughout history. We think that a working knowledge of what the prophets have said about the end of the world, as we now know it, is well advised. We think it is imperative.

The coming tribulation period seems to be in preparation today, and this is the first event on the timetable of the end of the world. The Lord Himself predicted such phenomena as famine, pestilence and earthquakes for this period, as well as the coming of false messiahs, the recovery and subsequent persecution of Israel and the rise of the world leader known as the antichrist (see all of Mt. 24, especially 24:21; related prophecy is found throughout Rev. 4 to 19 and throughout the Book of Daniel. Paul's warnings regarding the antichrist are given most definitively in 2 Thess. 2. Other epistles detail the "spirit of the antichrist.")

The "spirit of the antichrist" is already loose in the world, thinking people should see, and the family of mankind has seemed to reach new depths of depravity lately. Many prophecy scholars feel that our own times qualify well as leading very directly to the biblical end times.

The Rapture of the church is associated with this tribulation period. Scholars tend to place it before, during or after the seven-year tribulation, differing in subtleties of the scriptures, but all see it as the ultimate rescue of the church from the judgments to come upon the world. The authors follow the pretribulation view, literally expecting the Rapture at any moment (1 Thess. 5:9; Rev. 3:10).

The Rapture of the church is sudden. The Lord comes "as a thief in the night," "in the twinkling of an eye." Reservations for the Rapture must be made in advance!

The second coming of the Lord is scheduled at the end of the tribulation period. He will return to Jerusalem from where He'll rule the Kingdom. For 1,000 years the Lord and the believers will reign, while Satan is bound and the unbelievers await the final "Judgment Day" (Rev. 20). "Peace on earth, good will toward men" will at last prevail in this temporarily sorrowful world.

At the end of the Kingdom the Lord will judge all souls (except the believers who have gained forgiveness through the sacrifice of the Lord; the believers, in fact, will act as judges. The meek shall indeed "inherit the earth.")

And this is the time of the great final division of all mankind, every single one of which has been resurrected. Those who believe will join God for all eternity. Those who don't will remain in Hell for all eternity.

This, then, is the true, biblical life after death to be experienced by everyone. Of course the clinical experiences we related earlier don't begin to describe these myriad details, and they fail to deal with that all-important division of men into two eternal places. But suffice it to say that we will all live forever; we just need to choose the place.

Fortunately that choice remains open — "for a limited time only.."

ETERNITY AT A GLANCE

We can only "glance" at eternity because the idea is simply incomprehensible to us. The Bible gives some overall descriptions but not a great many of the details, presumably because men are not equipped, either by inclination or imagination, to appreciate eternity.

"Eternity" is God's name for this economy in which the earth and heaven are to be replaced. The city of

Jerusalem also figures into God's plan for this latter age; a "new heaven" a "new earth," and a "new Jerusalem" are all specified (Rev. 21:1-2).

Jerusalem is included in this wholly new order presumably as the seat of God's rule, as was its role in the past ages. Jerusalem was the sole site of the House of God, or the Temple, as it will be in the future!:

> Behold, the House of God is among men, and He shall dwell among them, and they shall be His people, and God Himself shall be among them, and He shall wipe away every tear from their eyes; and there shall no longer be any death; there shall no longer be any mourning, or crying or pain; the first things have passed away. And He who sits on the throne said, Behold I am making all things new (Rev. 21:3-5, NAS).

Isaiah specifies that even bad memories of the former ages will be abolished:

> For behold, I create new heavens and a new earth; and the former things shall not be remembered or come to mind. But be glad and rejoice forever in what I create (Isa. 65:17, NAS).

This, then, is heaven. There is no mention of people floating on fluffy clouds, plucking on harps or polishing their halos. That fable goes hand in hand with the red devil waving his pitchfork menacingly; both are the imaginings of men and not accurate to the scriptures.

We have descriptions of God's throne room in the Book of Revelation, and some idea of the bliss of the society of God's angels and servants. But the pearly gates, Peter standing by checking invitations, and all the rest of the storybook heaven do not appear.

All that we can imagine is that we become spiritual in nature, changed completely, needing the earth no more, at least in the form we see it now. We become truly one with God, but still retain our individuality — spiritual beings are distinct personalities and not one mass absorbed into God as in the tradition of the Eastern "Nirvana" concept. We are still who we are, but wonderfully re-created. The parallel usually suggested in nature is that of the simple larva emerging as the magnificent butterfly.

We can imagine, since it is specified in the scriptures that "God is love," that this will be a loving environment. Since He encourages us to love, peace, joy, beauty, we can imagine that we will eternally enjoy the presence of the very essence of all those most sublime feelings. We shall enjoy infinite love, infinite security and endless existence among those things. The glorious happiness to come is merely hinted at in the scriptures:

> Things which eye has not seen and ear has not heard, and which have not entered the heart of man, all that God has prepared for those who love Him! (1Cor. 2:9, NAS).

It is God's nature to give. He has given us all we have, and many things besides, which we do not yet perceive. We read that He loves us, but we can only wait for this coming age of eternity to experience the extent of that great love — "His great love with which He loved us...in order that in the ages to come He might show the surpassing riches of His grace in kindness toward us in Christ Jesus" (Eph. 2:7, NAS).

Jesus said simply, "Great is our reward in heaven" and Paul assures us "the sufferings of this present time are not worthy to be compared with the glory that is to be revealed to us" (Rom. 8:18 NAS).

The best part of all is that we will finally achieve the greatest blessing of the scriptures. We shall achieve the reality of which Nirvana, Perfect Virtue and Happiness, to mention a paltry few of man's ultimate goals, are the mere shadows.

We shall be "like Him" (1 Jn. 3:2, NAS).

What we keep falling short of now — the very likeness of Jesus Christ, the loving, sinless, perfect human being — will be our daily bread in eternity. We shall, each of us, be totally just, totally joyful, exceptionally powerful, totally pure. We will be with, talk with and constantly commune with God forever and ever. Time and space will no longer exist, but we will go on with the Maker of time and space infinitely.

We shall at that time understand everything — all of the secrets of the universe as explained by its Creator. We shall have our every question answered. And because God is infinite, there will be, throughout eternity, new things to learn of Him. Whatever we learn, we shall forever and ever, be mindful of the infinite love of God for us, expressed in the life, death, and resurrection of Christ.

We shall know the personalities of the Bible, our own friends and relatives who have joined us for eternity and our "guardian angels," as we think of them. The times of earthly spiritual and physical warfare will have passed as we enjoy perfect peace.

We shall be provided with immeasurable knowledge. We will comprehend everything. We shall inherit "the mind of Christ."

Paul utilized a breathtaking comparison in teaching his flock that it was unworthy for saved people to have favorites among their teachers. He used the following overwhelming expression:

> Therefore let no man glory in men. For all things are yours; whether Paul, or Apollos, or Cephas, or the world, or life, or death, or things present, or things to come; *all are yours*; And ye are Christ's; and Christ is God's! (1 Cor. 3:21-3, KJV).

The most confounding thing about eternity is the lack of *time*. We just can't imagine it. Time is our ongoing companion; our lives would be hopelessly confusing without this useful system of measurement.

137

But God will abolish it. That's the very essence of eternity; it has no time. It doesn't really last forever, since "forever" indicates timekeeping. It doesn't "last" at all, since "last" indicates a possibility of an end somewhere.

It just *is*. It always *is*. It infinitely *is*.

THE ACCEPTABLE TIME

But time is of the essence now in reserving a place for eternity.

Time plays a mighty role in our lives today. Time brings death, time passes as we consider God. Time goes by us as we ponder our lives, and time for living will run out of each of us in this world.

The Bible speaks to that:

> Behold, now is "the acceptable time"; behold, now is "the day of salvation"(2 Cor. 6:2, NAS).

We are writers, not preachers, but in a book of this nature, dealing with no less a matter of importance than life and death, we would feel remiss not to emphasize once again the way to eternity. Presumably any reader of this book is interested in life after death. We believe we have found it and we know it is available to anyone.

We realize that the popularity of the new life-after-death research is due to the intense interest all living people have in this ultimate matter. We feel that everyone alive would read the works of Moody, Kulber-Ross, etc., if they felt there was a grain of truth in them. We think that if people really believed they could prepare for death and ease the transition into the next life, they would line up at the doors of the mediums, the new clinics and the occult groups and clamor for a ticket. We think that if people really thought the next world were totally accepting of all souls, everyone would want to have one of those strange "clinical death" experiences immediately.

But, with all due respect, we think people are smarter than that.

We think people are very conscious of their shortcomings before God. We know from recent surveys that people in this nation are deeply concerned about God. We know that the Bible remains far and away the world's best-seller among all books, for all time, and that the faith of the Bible is by any measurement the dominant faith of man today.

We think every living human being wants to go to the Kingdom of God, and on to eternity with God. Some men have the means more easily than others, but among those who have the Bible and the basic knowledge of God required of men for salvation, we think everyone wants to come.

"Now is the acceptable time." In that there will be an end to this age and an end to this world, there's no reasonable alternative. Waiting on this decision is infinitely dangerous if we are to trust what the scriptures tell us. Such matters as the coming Armageddon are not matters of debate or indecision or interpretation. Those prophecies come from the very writings of those who prophesied the coming of Jesus Christ, the restoration of Israel in our time and a hundred other objective, plainly seen events in the story of man.

God is real, and He means what He says.

But God is love, and infinite mercy and forgiveness. How He has struggled for us! How He has tried to bring every man to salvation. Short of taking away our very freedom of choice, God has truly done His all.

Choose God. Go with Jesus Christ, Whose sacrifice provides your way.

"I am the way, the truth, and the life," He said (Jn. 14:6, KJV). "I am come that they might have life, and have it more abundantly" (Jn. 10:10, KJV).

If we made our point at all concerning the belief about death affecting the life led by an individual, then Jesus truly is "the life." Seek out a true believer and look at his life. The difference you'll see is Jesus. The Savior powers that successful life. Jesus will make that life eternal. That believer does not fear death, and thus he lives more fully.

The Savior knows you. There's no use taking a posture toward Jesus. He came here and He knows us all. "He knew the hearts of men," the gospel advises us. Considering all that He did on our behalf, won't you accept Him? Won't you close this matter once and for all, and guarantee yourself a place in the great ages to come?

Speak to Him now.

He is listening.

A simple, but sincere prayer like this is sufficient.

"Lord Jesus, I need you. Thank You for dying for my sins. I open the door of my life and receive you as my Savior and Lord. Thank You for forgiving all my sins. Take control of the center of my life. Make me the kind of person You want me to be."

If you prayed that prayer, Welcome to eternity! And we highly recommend that you read Hal Lindsey's *The Liberation of Planet Earth* which explains what a new believer needs to know about his new life and growth in Christ.

10

The Great Hope

Probably everyone who has read this book hopes to live forever. This is undoubtedly the great hope of human existence.

We want to go on. We want to *live*. We want to be happy and gratified, both in this life and in the next one.

We search for a way to the next live — which is what the life-after-death research is really all about — and we search for guarantees that it won't be all over for each of us when we die.

The Bible gives people the great hope of life after death, and men who do not read the Bible have been trying in various ways to provide for this fundamental hope. If we knew — *really knew* — that death would not be the end for us, what a different life this would be. If we could find out that we are going to a better place — a better life — in the beyond, this human life would take on a new dimension of peace and joy. If only we really knew!

It was the author's intention in this book to shed some light on this ultimate question of human existence. By looking at the new theories of life after death, and the Bible, with its older but ever trustworthy information, we hoped to clarify a difficult subject. If the matter has been somewhat confusing, that's hard to avoid. Everyone at work in such an area of mystery must deal with some very hard questions.

In this final chapter we will restate what we have said briefly, to pull the whole subject together, and then we will say a last word about our choice of positions on this vital matter. We favor the biblical position, it is no secret, and we have hopefully justified our choice.

Probably our position will meet with a lot of opposition. People *don't want* to disbelieve the new life-after-death stories. These accounts give an answer, of a kind at least, for one of our most important longings. And biblical positions on *anything* have never been popular with the majority of mankind.

This has been a necessarily involved and complex book, due to the subject matter, and a general recap of what has been said seems in order. Probably the authors have tended to polarize readers with this kind of study. We have taken a very definite position on a matter where not very definite information is available. We have, on the strength of the scriptures and certain weaknesses in the clinical death reports, declared the majority of cases of life after death to be a demonic deception. Some readers may by this time be very satisfied with our position; others may think we're "dead" wrong. This final chapter may help moderate things on that score, plus encourage what the Bible refers to as "the great hope" of the believers.

In our initial chapters we gave the reports of the new life-after-death experiences exactly as they have been publicly presented. We introduced the various researchers who have contributed to this unique new field of study, and we discussed what we conceived of as the new American way of death. In an unbiased way, we hope, we laid out the evidence and the atmosphere into which it has emerged.

Then we discussed some of the new difficulties doctors and laymen alike are presently experiencing in trying to define death. We spoke of the remarkable resuscitation techniques now being utilized to prolong life, and how they tend to make more uncertain the diagnosis of death. We meant to cast a certain doubt on the ''clinical death'' reports, the best of the life-after-death cases, and we feel that this doubt is justified.

Then we critically examined some of the more complete reports from the beyond, with a view to understanding phenomena like the Being of Light, the ''review'' of the subject's life, the encountering of friends and relatives in the beyond, and so forth. We found some reportedly negative experiences with life after death and we detected a pervasive influence of the occult running through the cases in general.

In ''Spiritual Warfare'' and ''The Satan Factor,'' we illustrated the rather surprising tie-ins of the occult world to this particular research. We uncovered a ''psychic bias,'' if we may call it that, in the research, involving both the experimenters and their materials. We offered some comparisons between today's occultic activities, like the out-of-the-body trips many people are taking, and the life-after-death reports. We cited biblical materials relevant to the issue of demonic activity. We noted that the nether forces, the devil, or whatever the reader prefers to think of as the negative side of the ongoing spiritual battle, would reasonably be expected to pass out ''good news'' and masquerade as the Being of Light, the friendly spirits, etc. We showed that scientists are seriously operating a clinic which purports to teach people an advantageous way of dying and traveling to the next world.

Finally we went to the Bible and demonstrated God's plan for eternal life via salvation through Christ. We found a long list of discrepancies between the scriptural picture of life after death and the clinical reports — so many that it would be difficult, we feel, for a believer in

God to find validity in the new research. We illustrated the biblical plan of salvation as clearly as space would allow, and we recommended it.

Probably the chief objection to our position would be in the fact that we rely so heavily on the scriptures to discount the life-after-death reports. After all, the reports are happening in the here-and-now. They can be seen — the people can be interviewed. Those who have come back from clinical death are available to us, whereas the prophets and the Lord Himself departed this earth long ago.

We would say to that objection that the matter can be tested. We feel that any person who has the slightest doubt about where he will go upon death, or whether he will really go anywhere at all, should test this matter. The evidence for the divine inspiration and the reliability of the Scripture is available to all.[1] Read the Gospels seriously — critically, if you want, but honestly.

And we think it stands to reason that every living person should make some sort of decision on this issue.

BORN AGAIN!

We have mainly utilized the scriptures for their information about the "hereafter," rather than the "here." A word should be said, before we conclude this book, about what one gains *in this life* by being "born again."

The term "born again" has recently received a great boost by the media. A valid biblical concept (John 3, et al), it has always been regarded as a bit of an overstatement by those on the outside looking in. Many people will give due credit for the lives led by devout Christians, the effective charities, the missionary endeavors and all the rest of the good works of biblically committed people. But that the believers were so inspired as to be termed "born again" was generally more than worldly people would swallow. The very term seemed too far-out. But now we have a professing born-again believer in the news daily and the term is gaining currency.

Well and good. It's the correct term because the true believer really is reborn, biblically.

The transformation that occurs in any person when he really encounters Jesus Christ is nothing short of amazing. The drug-addiction cures, the healings, the rescues from alcoholism, prostitution and crime of all sorts aside, the average everyday human being seems to experience something utterly miraculous with this faith in Christ. Psychologists and behavioral scientists of every discipline are impressed, however grudgingly, at the change that comes over new converts to Christianity. This dominant religion of today's world, has undoubtedly had a profound effect on the history of politics, science and human relations throughout the ages since the Master walked the earth. Millions have drunk of the Lord's "living water" (Jn. 4) and come away satisfied, never thirsting again.

Trying to make out just what occurs within the human psyche when conversion changes a life, behaviorists have conceded that the experience of the forgiveness of sin is very important. Human beings change when they fully perceive that God indeed does love them — each and every one — and is willing, on the basis of Christ's sacrifice, to fully forgive their sins. Unrelenting guilt seems to be a universal disability of the human condition and Christian conversion undoubtedly relieves it.

More simply, we prosper when we know that we serve a loving God and our conscience becomes clear when we realize what He has done for us. The cross, so heavy for the Lord to bear, lightens the lives of everyone else. There is no way to overstate that feeling and no way to get it somewhere else. Any believer will readily testify to it and will be happy to share it with the willing listener.

But it's not just a matter of having a good conscience that makes the life here and now so pleasing and peaceful for the believer. Actually, the worldwide mission of serving Christ Himself is still more exhilarating. To be cleansed is a good thing; to be then called into gratifying and fulfilling service is a truly *wonderful* thing!

It causes some wonder among unbelievers that Christians don't "drop out." People drop out of all walks of life — businessmen opt for a farm; athletes, weary of the competition, retire before their time; youngsters drop out of school, out of their homes and, these days, almost out of this world; the rich commit suicide all the time. People get fed up, even with the best of things sometimes, and they quit. But it's extremely difficult to discover a Christian "de-convert" anywhere. Nobody ever says, "I walked with Christ for awhile but then I didn't believe anymore."

They must be getting something that really lasts. Considering the pains they go through — the derision, the sacrifices often called for by the Lord, the lives of steady service only to be rewarded in the life to come — they really must be *enjoying* the here-and-now.

And the fact is, they are. The Christian life which begins at the moment of salvation only gets better. This is a biblical promise, in fact. The beliver lives fruitfully,

> Being confident of this very thing, that He which hath began a good work in you will perform it until the day of Jesus Christ (Phil. 1:6, KJV).

Until the day of the return of the Lord the believer will constantly enjoy the very works of God in his life. And then, as we have seen, the never-ending life with God will commence—the ultimate "Life After Death."

Even without this supernatural effect of God actually operating in the life of the believer, the very identification with the Lord brings great satisfaction to the believer. Who among the philosophers of the world can compare with Christ? Who had His mind, His heart, His compassion? Who addressed themselves so accurately and pointedly to the real human condition? Who else could stand here on earth and promise life after death to every one of us?

There are *unbelievers* who deeply respect the mind of Christ. Secular historians invariably give Him His due place at the very center of human history. Filmmakers, novelists and playwrights seek to somehow capture the glory of the Lord in secularized versions of the gospel that still, adulterated as they usually are, inspire the public invariably. Most of those in the helping professions very profoundly appreciate the humane teachings and the supreme example of sacrifice provided by the Carpenter of Galilee.

But how much better it is to really know Him — to dwell with Him constantly!

The believer is truly in this position: he has a wonderful life now, supernaturally managed and guaranteed fruitful; and he has a wonderful life to come, in the very presence of God and guaranteed forever.

We have talked about life after death in all of its latest manifestations and philosophies throughout this book. It's surely time now to praise the life *before* death available to those born again. As we explained in the preceding chapter, this remarkable and fulfilling life is free for the asking. God shuts no one out who will come to Him.

And that's part of our testing procedure. We offered above that anyone having any remaining question about life after death should conduct a test. If the out-of-the-body travel clinic is the answer then the Bible is wrong. If God is the answer then the occult powers will simply lose another battle.

Every person will make a choice, sooner or later. We urge you, under the circumstances, to make yours immediately.

Is there life after death?

There certainly is.

Be born again and you'll enjoy it forever!

1. Good beginners books are: Vos (ed.) *Can I Trust the Bible?*; Wenham, *Christ and the Bible*; J. W. Montgomery, *History and Christianity*; M. Green, *Runaway World*; C. Pinnock, *Set Forth Your Case*.

   More advanced books include: J. W. Montgomery, *Christianity for the Tough Minded*; F. Schaeffer, *He Is There and He Is Not Silent*; *The God Who Is There*; J. W. Montgomery, *Where Is History Going?* (2 Vols.); W. Smith, *Therefore Stand*; C. Pinnock, *Biblical Revelation*; as well as the books referred to in the text.

   For a book on the Biblical view of death, G. C. Studer, *After Death, What?* (*Herald Press*, 1976).

NOTES